Things Happen for a Reason

Things Happen for a Reason

Published by Frog, Ltd.
Frog, Ltd. books are distributed by:
North Atlantic Books
P. O. Box 12327
Berkeley, CA 94712

Library of Congress Cataloging-in-Publication Data
Leach, Terry, 1954-
   Things happen for a reason: the true story of an itinerant life in baseball/by Terry Leach and Tom Clark.
      p. cm.
ISBN 1-58394-050-2 (alk. paper)
   1. Leach, Terry, 1954- 2. Baseball players--United States--Biography. 3. Pitchers (Baseball)--United States--Biography. I. Clark, Tom, 1941- II. Title.

GV865.L35 A3 2000
796.357'092--dc21
[B]   99-086103

Book cover and interior designed by Carolina de Bartolo.

Printed in the United States of America.
Distributed to the book trade by Publishers Group West.

1 2 3 4 5 6 7 8 9 / 03   02 01 00

Things Happen for a Reason

The True Story of an Itinerant Life in Baseball

Terry Leach with Tom Clark

Frog, Ltd.
Berkeley, California

To T. L.

Congrats on the perfect "10." It's been an absolute pleasure catching you during your streak and always. Continued success throughout your career and may the Lord's blessings continue to guide and protect you and yours always.

Catch ya later, your pal

Gary Carter

Contents

Dedication

In my life I have been blessed by being surrounded by a great family, really good friends and nice people. It would have been really hard to go wrong in life with such wonderful people and role models as my mother, Alma, and father, Cecil. They gave me everything I ever needed physically, and all the love, encouragement, and backing that I could have ever asked for.

I owe a tremendous amount of thanks and appreciation to my wife Chris for supporting me throughout my professional career. Even though she admits to not being a fan of the baseball life, she took care of me, encouraged me, defended me, and although it meant my being away longer, prayed for me to be able to fulfill my dreams of pitching in a World Series.

To her I give a special dedication and love.

PS: All my love to Savannah.

Preface by David Cone

The ebbs and flows of two young pitchers trying to establish themselves on the defending world-champion 1986 New York Mets served as the backdrop for what has become a close friendship between two men.

It was in 1987, as we both competed for rare and precious spots on the great Mets' pitching staff, that I first met Terry Leach. Little did we hopefuls foresee that, as the '87 season began to unfold, injuries would decimate the entire starting rotation to such a degree that Terry and I would go, seemingly overnight, from longshots to mainstays.

First, Doc Gooden went on the disabled list — substance-abuse. Roger McDowell's hernia was followed by Rick Aguilera's elbow surgery. The next victim was Sid Fernandez with arm woes; Bobby Ojeda made his trip to list with a bum knee.

The carnage did not end there. Ron Darling succumbed to a torn ligament in his thumb. I was next in line for a spot in the rotation, and I did get in five major-league starts before the hex looked my way. I came off being drilled with a pitch from San Francisco's Atlee Hammaker with a shattered finger.

It was only then that Terry got his shot in the Mets' rotation. Little may have been expected of him, but everyone who knew the guy's heart and what he had inside him wasn't surprised. This so-called Triple-A pitcher promptly took us all on a ride rarely seen in baseball history.

They once said of Brooks Robinson that he played like a guy who came down from a higher league. Well, Terry didn't have Brooks' kind of raw talent, but he sure came from somewhere none of us had ever heard of before. It was as astonishing as if an unknown Elvis had just taken the mound and tossed "Hound Dog" and "Heartbreak Hotel" in succession, right out of his hat impromptu, no warning. Then followed it up with "Jailhouse Rock" and "Don't Be Cruel." And still wasn't halfway done. No way, Terry!

Ten straight victories from the Southern gentleman out of Selma, Alabama. Ten pretty-much monster games. Ten masterpieces worthy of a crafty vet. It was easily the feel-good story of the year in Major League Baseball.

To a man, our clubhouse was filled with admiration and hope as Terry carried the pitching staff — in fact, the entire team — through the dog days of summer back into the pennant race.

It wasn't just Terry's pitching success but rather the manner in which he carried himself, both on and off the field. He was a friend and an example to everyone around him, equally in adversity and success.

Terry supported us. We knew that, and we rooted for him too. This wasn't the usual player cheerleading on the bench. He was a colleague and buddy, a man whose actions were true as his words. At the same time that he was teaching a master class on the mound, he was a cut-up of the highest order, truly a funny guy. The feeling between him and his teammates was most certainly mutual and contagious. Quite simply Terry is one of the best teammates I've ever been around.

Terry's sense of responsibility and respect for the grand game of baseball continues at present, as he has become a caring and supportive teacher. He gives lessons the way he played, with love and attention. Just as he once made us all better players and people for being his teammates, he is building great confidence in fledgling kids, making them better players of the game or on whatever path life takes them. They will carry Terry's special imprint — high spirit and grace under fire — into every league in which they one day play.

You can now follow Terry along the incredible grind of his path to the big leagues. You can be with him amid the high and unique humor of the Major League clubhouse. And you can share his graceful exit from the pros to that sometimes unheralded but still very special school in which we players of the game get to pass on our heritage to the generations after us.

— David Cone
New York Yankees

Introduction by Paul Auster

I remember him well. A stocky right-hander with a sidearm delivery who wore number 26. Not much speed, but a tricky combination of sliders and sinkers that kept the hitters off balance: "give them a little air to mash at." He started when called upon, pitched in long relief, worked as a set-up man, intermittently served as a closer. When he was with the New York Mets, his teammates called him Jack. As in Jack-of-All-Trades. Whatever he was asked to do, he did. He might not have impressed you, but he rarely failed to get the job done.

Terry Leach was never a star. He struggled in the minor leagues for many years before he was given a chance, and even when he performed well, his efforts often went unnoticed. In a late season start for the Mets in 1982, he pitched a one-hit, ten-inning shutout against the Phillies, but the following year he was back in the minors. As an undrafted player with an unorthodox style and less than overpowering natural skills, he had to work harder that everyone else to win a place for himself. He survived on guts, humor, and an irrational love of the game. He simply refused to take no for an answer, and in the end he built a solid career for himself. How many pitchers have had ten-game winning streaks and a season's record of 11-1? How many pitchers have come into a World Series game to face the opposing team's hottest hitter with two outs and the bases loaded and managed to strike that hitter out? Terry Leach did those things, and by the time you read about them in this short but infinitely charming book, you have already learned that this man is more than just an ex-pitcher. He is a born story teller, and with Tom Clark's help he has put together one of the most enjoyable baseball books I have read in years.

I saw Terry Leach pitch many times, but only once in person. It was a warm August night in 1985, and at the last minute my wife and I decided to go out to Shea Stadium to watch the Mets play against the Giants. We got there just before the game began, bought our tickets at the game, and hustled up to our seats in the right-center-field mezzanine — just in time for the National Anthem. Sid

Fernandez was supposed to be pitching against Vida Blue that night, but Fernandez came down sick while warming up on the mound and had to be scratched. Terry Leach was sitting in the clubhouse at that moment, dressed in his underwear and working on a crossword puzzle. Five minutes later, he threw the first of 87 pitches he would throw that night. That averages out to fewer than ten pitches an inning over nine innings, a number that signifies absolute mastery over the other team. Since Terry Leach went the full nine innings, shutting out the Giants on just 3 hits, I would have to rank his performance as the greatest one I have ever had the pleasure to witness. The Giants couldn't touch him. Late in the game, when he laid down a successful sacrifice bunt, Terry Leach was given the first standing ovation of his Major League career. My wife and I were standing with that crowd. We were both clapping, and we were both shouting our heads off. Even now, fourteen and a half years later, we still talk about that night as the most perfect night of baseball we have ever had.

— Paul Auster
December 18, 1999

Part One
Early Years

Starting Out

I don't remember a first moment when I started playing baseball. I remember little things, like going out in the back yard and playing some catch with my dad. Maybe it's because I teach baseball to kids now that I remember him teaching me how to play catch. I was just a little kid, I didn't even know how to catch a ball. He showed me how to turn my glove down when the ball was coming in below my waist and turn my glove up when it was coming in above. We'd make a game out of it: If I didn't hold my glove right, I'd have to take a lap around the yard. And you know, that will make a boy concentrate. I remember working hard on that little trick of keeping my glove turned right. I couldn't have been any more than six years old, but playing ball was already a serious thing to me.

I was the little guy in the bunch — I had two brothers who were quite a bit older. Billy, who passed away a few years ago, was fourteen years older than me, and Alan is seven years older. Both of those boys were very athletic, and so, since I was always wanting to be hanging out with them and their friends, I always felt I had to be a little bit tougher and better than a typical kid my age. My brother Alan, in particular, was at home a lot, and he'd have his buddies over, playing this and that. And here I'd be, seven years younger, trying to keep up. If it was football, say, here'd be three of them lined up, I'd be carrying the ball, and I'd have to run through them without getting tackled. Of course most of the time I failed at it. That's the way it always was. Being younger pushed me to be a little bit better. Then if I failed, I still got the benefits. Being at a disadvantage can work for you if you take your failures and learn from them.

I was always trying to keep up with the older guys in my neighborhood at baseball, too. Sometimes that was hard, but I know now that it helped me a lot just to always keep on trying. Perseverance definitely proved to be an important asset for me, later on, when I was playing baseball to make a living.

Scared to Death

I grew up in Selma, Alabama. I started playing baseball in back yards in my neighborhood, before I was old enough for Little League. It was a great neighborhood for getting a game up. One family had five boys. We must have had fifteen, sixteen, seventeen boys in that immediate neighborhood — sometimes we could get up nine to a side, just playing in a yard. I first went over to the Little League Park to play in 1963, when I was nine years old. I was asked to play on a team sponsored by a local Chevrolet dealer. A nine-year-old kid on a team that had ten-, eleven-, twelve-year-olds. I was the youngest kid on the team, and I was scared to death.

I remember being scared to death every time that Little League team played. I played centerfield. I just didn't think I belonged out there. Other kids, if it rained and we got rained out, they'd actually cry, that's how bad they wanted to play those games. Myself, I'd be relieved when we were rained out. I'd be happy, because then I wouldn't be under that pressure to go out in centerfield and perform.

At that stage baseball scared me, because I felt like I should always do well. In baseball you don't always do well, but I didn't know that yet. I was afraid I wasn't good enough. But there were two plays that I made that helped me get over the hump, to get past some of my fears and start to build up my confidence and my belief in myself, that I could actually play this game. One time, playing infield in a pickup game at a summer camp, playing third base, I dove and caught a ball, diving flat out on my belly as I raced toward home plate. And then, in a Little League game, I made a leaping catch. I jumped up and caught a ball over the wall. I always considered that my greatest and most outstanding play as a centerfielder. Anyway it sure felt good to know I could do something right. Just those two little moments — the feeling that I got when I made those two plays — spurred me on to stick with the game, at that point. I think that feeling kept me playing.

And I was always big and strong and fast, compared to the other kids around where I lived. In fact, I could play the game pretty well, so in some ways it's kind of funny that as a kid it always scared me so much.

I don't know where that pressure came from. My parents didn't make me play Little League. They didn't demand things out of me — I did. My dad had played football at Auburn. He had learned things there that made him understand it's important not to put pressure on anyone. My parents didn't push me to do anything. In fact, even though growing up in Alabama everybody's major objective was to play football either for Auburn or for Alabama, my dad didn't want me to play high school football until I got to the eleventh or twelfth grade. And since there were still moments when I didn't think I was ever going to be a baseball player, at that point it was really football that I had in mind. I thought I was going to play fullback at Auburn. Tucker Frederickson, who used to play for the New York Giants, was a fullback from Auburn, and that's who I was modeling myself on.

As I say I had always been pretty big for my age. But then as I got a little bit older the other kids started to be just as big or bigger. And high school football soon convinced me I didn't like getting hurt. That's what inclined me toward baseball, finally, getting clipped in a high school football practice. As I mentioned, my dad didn't want me going out for the team, because he thought I was still too young, my legs and all weren't developed enough. My dad was a cotton buyer at that time. During the cotton season he'd go out of town on Mondays and get back on Fridays. One Monday he left and that same day I went out for football. During that week I made the starting team. By Friday, when he got back home for the weekend, I was in a cast practically from the top of my head down to my toes. He said, "I told you." Daddy never got mad about things like that. In fact my mom Alma and dad Cecil are two of the mellowest people around. But that was it for me and football.

First Pitching Experiences

I must have been eleven years old when I started pitching. When I was in the fourth grade or so, about ten years old, I broke my heel. After that I didn't get to play any sports for a year. Couldn't play football, baseball, anything — couldn't run. We'd run around barefoot a lot down in Alabama, just boys playing, and that's how it happened. We'd build these play houses, and jump off them. Well, I loved doing that, but then I broke a bone in my heel doing it. And you know, it was almost like I started an epidemic, because a couple of my friends came up with that same injury, doing that same fool thing. There's a little crescent-shaped bone there in the back of your heel, and when you're young that bone's not developed very much, so it's really fragile. We were always jumping around barefooted, and we just cracked those bones. Mine took a year to mend. For a long time after that I could take off running just fine, but when I would try to stop, I couldn't put any weight on my heel, I had to walk on my toes. It was just killing me, and I had to take a year off, no baseball or anything. And then when I came back, I had a new idea — I wanted to be a pitcher. So at eleven years old I started pitching a little bit.

I was successful at pitching right away, just because I could throw hard. Like I said, I was big and strong — at that point still a little bigger and stronger than your average eleven or twelve year old. In fact when I first started pitching I could throw the ball extremely hard, so that most of those kids were a little bit scared to stand up at the plate against me. Plus I didn't have very good control. I hit people, and that really made it a case where nobody wanted to dig in when I was out there throwing. I remember one time, I hit a friend of mine, Phaton Gwynn was his name, three times in one game. He showed up the next day with bruises all up and down his side. Well, maybe Phaton getting hit at least protected some of the other people from me, because I don't think I hit anybody else during that particular game. I hit Phaton the first time, and then I was a little worried about it after that. But just because that thought was planted in my mind, I nailed him two or three more times. I guess it was some unconscious thing. We were still in Little League then, couldn't have been more than eleven or twelve. But little things like that do stick with you.

And you know, there's a little happy ending to that story, too, because about twenty years later Phaton Gwynn came up to New York one time and saw me play with the Mets. I got him into the game, and afterwards he came down in the clubhouse and we all talked to him. But during the game he was up there in the stands, hollering and rooting for me. That was pretty neat. It was like a reward: I all but killed him that day in Little League, but then I got to take him to a game in the big leagues twenty years later.

A Taste of What Everything Is

So now I was a pitcher; but also part of the time I was a catcher, plus I played some third base, and a little first base now and then as well. From Little League on, I always liked pitching best, but I also liked hitting a whole lot too. If I'd been allowed to stay with it, I might have turned out a fair hitter. I've hit one or two shots in my time. One summer while I was at Auburn I went down to Birmingham after the college season with our rightfielder, Steve Rea, and my catcher, Tommy Morton, and we all played in a game down there. Those guys were both good hitters, but I think I really surprised them by going deep not once but twice in that game. And another time around then, '75 or so, I won an extra-inning exhibition all-star game in Johnstown, Pa., with a walkoff piece against Mark Fidrych. Took him deep over that great big old outfield wall. Later on when I was down with the Mets Triple-A team at Tidewater and Mark had signed with the Red Sox and was playing with their Triple-A team at Pawtucket, we met up again. We had a good laugh about it. Pitchers always take a special joy in hitting home runs, but they really hate giving them up to other pitchers.

I'll admit right here I was never much of a hitter in the big leagues. Zero ninety-seven lifetime batting average, zero lifetime home runs. Then again, in eleven years I totaled exactly seventy-two big league at bats. Who knows what kind of hitter I'd have become if I'd had a chance to learn hitting? Now you're probably thinking, that's what every pitcher who ever had a lifetime average under a buck will tell you. But I led my high school team in home runs and batting average. Batted cleanup my senior year. In fact I was a good enough hitter that I actually went to college as a third baseman. But when I got to Auburn they decided they needed pitching, so they turned me into a pitcher. And after my freshman year, college baseball adopted the designated hitter rule. From then on I never really got to swing a bat regularly any more, never got a chance to develop as a hitter.

I think that's a big part of the reason why, in teaching baseball to younger kids now, I'm really against imposing the designated hitter rule on them too early. Especially at the high school level, I think it's wrong. I go to a lot of high school games now, they're all using the designated hitter. I see scouts at these games. The guy the scouts are looking at is the best athlete, and that's most often going to be one of the pitchers. From Little League on, the best athlete on your team usually also happens to be a kid who can throw the ball a little better than anybody else. It's only natural. And naturally he's the one you're going to put on the mound to be your pitcher. But now, once that kid gets up to high school, he's never again going to get a chance to hit; he'll never develop his skills as a hitter. I think it's way too early for any youngster to have to specialize like that, it limits his possibilities too much.

To correct that, I'd suggest that if you're going to have a designated hitter, have ten men in your lineup. Let your pitcher hit, and then throw in an extra DH too, if you want to keep hitting as a specialized role. And then later, in college, I really think everybody should be expected to do everything, to hit as well as play the field. That way a young player not only equips himself against the misfortune of an injury or deficit of skill at the position he may have originally chosen, but learns the totality of the game. Of course, that's going to be even more important to him if he intends to make the game his life.

A young player should be well-rounded. That's how we teach kids in the baseball camps we give now. A kid will show up and say, "I'm a second baseman." He's ten years old, and he knows he's a second baseman. We say, "Nope. While you're with us, you're going to do everything. You're going to be all over this field." But then every time we start them playing full-scale games, they'll start raising their hands again, "I want to play second!" Well, as teachers, we just hate that. At that point, where they think they want to play is the last place we're going to put them. Before we do that we'll move them all around the field, just to let them get a taste of what everything is.

Maybe in that respect baseball's not too different from anything else in life. You're always moving around and having to try new things and you never know what's coming, so it's probably a good idea to be prepared for a little of everything.

Part Two
Auburn

A Three-Quarters Ride

I had a little taste of success at an early stage. I made the Selma High School baseball team as a freshman. Played in the Dixie Senior League for three years. We ended up being runner-up in the Dixie Senior World Series in '69, and then in '71 we won it, playing back home in Selma. In '72, when I graduated from Selma High, Auburn University offered me a partial scholarship.

I was real happy about getting to go to Auburn, but the problem was, I did not get a full scholarship. My friend Mickey Miller, who was also from Selma, went to Auburn that same year on a full scholarship, but I only got a three-quarters ride. The school paid for basically everything but my food, which would have been all right if you didn't have to eat to play baseball. Housing was taken care of, and tuition and books — the only thing I didn't get was eating. But at Auburn that was a pretty big deal, because in the athletic dorm there they ate real good. You see, Auburn is big football. They had lobster nights, steak nights.... If you were on the teams, they took care of you, they had your prime food over there. And here I was, still growing. I thought it would be good to waste no time in getting myself moved up to a full scholarship. And during my first year I was promised that if I contributed to the team in any way, that's just what would happen.

Well, in my sophomore year, 1974, I went 9-0, with an earned run average of 1.30 — just over one earned run per nine innings. In terms of sheer numbers, that was definitely the best year I've ever had anywhere on this planet. I believe a lot of my records from that year are still in the Auburn record books. It may not be the very best year anybody's ever had pitching at Auburn, but it's up there in the top four or five. After having a season like that I definitely felt like I deserved a place at the table on lobster night or steak night. Sure enough, when the next season was coming around, I got called into the head coach's office. They were starting to enforce these new

NCAA rules, the coach told me. Whatever kind of scholarship you'd signed up for, now it turned out that's the kind you were stuck with for your whole four years. "That's the new rule now and you've got to live with it."

Well, that sure wasn't what they'd been telling me all along. I was plenty ticked off. I'd had a real fine year and had helped out the team. I had been promised something, that thing had been taken away from me. That's how I looked at it, at the time.

My dad was a little bit upset about this too. Well, not just a little bit — quite a bit. He had his own history with that school. He had gone to Auburn to play football many years ago, when Coach Shug Jordan was there. Shug Jordan was one of the top football coaches ever at Auburn, rated right up there with the nation's best in his time. Shug also hailed from Selma, which down there was considered a little feather in our cap. But back when my dad went to Auburn on a football scholarship, if you got hurt and could no longer play, they could just take your scholarship away from you. And that's what had happened to him. He'd hurt his knee, he couldn't play, he'd lost his scholarship because of it, and afterwards he always held Coach Shug Jordan partly responsible. After he got hurt Shug Jordan questioned his effort, and cut him from the team. But that's not the way my dad is, he never quit or dogged it in his life. He felt Shug Jordan had mistreated him, that was his own deeper history with Auburn. Mind you, my dad had gone on and done well and had a good life, had supported us and taken care of us. But he'd never stopped feeling bitter about the way that scholarship he'd earned had been taken away from him.

And now here I was getting my own shot at a full scholarship and having it taken away from me even though we knew I'd earned it. You can guess my dad got pretty heated. He was ready to take me out of that school right there and then. In fact he went out and just about got me signed up at South Alabama, where Eddie Stanky was coaching. I had originally considered South Alabama before coming to Auburn. Now we were talking about my going down there to try out and if things went okay, I'd go ahead and transfer.

But meanwhile I'd been doing some of my own thinking about all this. And the one thing that was prominent in my mind was the fact that at that time Auburn had a very fine baseball team. So I told my dad that. I said, "This team has been together for a few years, it's actually the best team in the South right now and it's got a chance to be awesome. I really don't think I ought to leave just yet. No, I'd like to just stay on a while and see things out."

High Notes, Low Notes

That ended up being a pretty good decision on my part. I stuck it out for four years at Auburn. In the winter after my junior year my name came up in a little supplementary major league draft they had back then — Boston picked me in the seventh round, offered me a couple of thousand dollars which wouldn't even have got me through the school year, then pulled back their offer when they found out I was ineligible for that draft after all, due to being overage. I went back for my senior year, and that year the Auburn team lived up to the expectations I'd had.

We won the Southeastern Conference championship, and then went to the South Regional Playoffs, where we faced Tennessee, Jacksonville University and Florida State and beat all three of them. That got us into the College World Series, a real big thing for us — only the second time that Auburn had ever been there, in all the years they'd been playing baseball at that school. We went on to the Series, and unfortunately we did not do as well as we had anticipated. We were eliminated in the first round after getting beat twice. But we still finished up that year on a pretty high note, just getting that far. We had great guys and a fine team, and I was glad I'd stayed.

So though I'd gone to college as third baseman, I never actually played third base there. When I got to Auburn I found out they already had an outstanding third baseman. That's when they made a pitcher out of me. The guy who was playing third when I got there was a senior, and he was such a fine player that I was really surprised when he was not drafted after he graduated. Never drafted — which I couldn't understand, I always thought he should have had a shot. But in fact we had a number of people on that team who I felt deserved a chance to keep on playing. Our second baseman, Mickey Miller, the boy from Selma, he actually was the top dog on that team, he was never drafted either. Mick was number one on that Auburn team, and I was never better than number two. Everybody thought Mickey was going to make it, and he should have, but things just didn't work out for him. I remember in Little League, high school ball, he was always just a step ahead of me, and in college too, he was always a cut above. But then after our senior year neither one of us got drafted by a major league team. We didn't get picked, that was just the way it was.

Streaking

Several interesting things happened to me when I was in college. You might say those years were a broadening experience. It was a funny era, too. Things that went on were probably not the same things that happen today at colleges. Streaking, for example, was a very big thing at Auburn around then. Streaks were constantly going on, all over campus. Some of them were staged: Somebody would call you and tip you off, and you would go on over to campus and check out the action. But then again a streak might just break out all of a sudden, out of the blue. It was unbelievable. One day I was standing out on the mound pitching a game for the Auburn baseball team when all of a sudden I noticed a commotion off to my left, and I heard a scream. I looked over and here comes a guy and a girl, streaking toward me out of foul territory from over behind first base. They came across the infield, passed right by where I stood on the pitcher's mound and then headed over shortstop all the way out into left field and out the gate. Well, that was the Seventies. I remember the girl had on just one thing, a red bandana. Later she came back into the stands, and everybody gave her a standing ovation.

By the way, the streaking that day didn't throw my game off one bit. I struck out the next hitter on three pitches. When I was pitching I always liked having a little something different happening, to spur me on.

The Baseball Fraternity

Generally speaking I had a pretty fine time in college. I wasn't in a fraternity. Didn't see any need to join one. I went to all the different rush parties every year — not exactly rushing, but just went. We'd all just show up. Hey, why join? You can still go to all the parties. I didn't see any need to join anything, the baseball team was its own fraternity. Most of us just hung out with each other. And we all each had our own different friends from our various different towns, so that made a pretty big collection of people right there. And we all got along very well together. We'd all go to all the parties. Everybody belonged to everything. Oh, I was into everything in those years. I was still getting rushed by fraternities at Auburn when I was a senior. I had friends from Selma who were in Kappa Alpha, that was one of the big fraternities with the Selma guys. Those boys would still be bringing me in, though I was never going to pledge there. We'd all go have a drink with them. After football games it was just wonderful, we'd all go anywhere, everybody always had bands, and I could bring my friends from the baseball team with me just about everywhere.

Unwilling Punter

Though I didn't play football at Auburn, I guess you could say I had one close call. For a little while I dated an assistant football coach's daughter. Coach Davis was his name. One night I was over at their house and got to talking with him. The team was having trouble with their punters, he said. The guys they had kicking for them just couldn't get any distance out of their punts. Now I could kick a football barefooted — like I said, as boys in Selma we'd accustomed ourselves to doing just about everything barefoot. So talking to Coach Davis, something made me pipe up, "Heck, Coach, I sure can kick a football forty yards for you, if you'll just let me do it bare-foot." That turned out not to have been the smartest thing I've ever said. The next thing I knew, Coach Davis came to me and said, "You know, son, I mentioned what you said to Shug Jordan." I just about dropped dead on the spot. Now here's Shug Jordan, the same man who cut my dad from the Auburn football team — good gracious, what was it, twenty, thirty years ago? And now I had a vision of two-hundred-and-forty-pound guys running at me and crushing me for Shug Jordan's sake. "No thanks," I told Coach Davis. "I had enough of that in high school." And Coach Davis said, "You know, Shug asked me if your daddy's name was Cecil." Here Shug Jordan had remembered my dad's name over all those years. Could it be that what he'd done had actually stayed with him a little bit after all? "Yeah, that's my daddy's name," I said. Coach Davis said, "Well, Shug remembers your daddy." Next time I spoke to my dad I said, "Daddy, would you like to come up and see Shug Jordan some-time?" He said, "No, I've really got no desire ever to see that man."

Running

I was talking lately with Tommy Morton, who was my catcher at Auburn. Tommy reminded me how he and Mickey Miller used to get on me when we were all doing our running. Oh my, we used to do some running at Auburn! We'd be doing our laps of the field and those guys would be running along there behind me, just cracking up. Because every step it looked like I was just about to drop! I could hear them kidding around about whether I was going to make it to the end of the lap. But somehow or other I always managed to stay out there a little bit ahead of them. And I usually finished up those runs in prime time, even though the whole way it probably looked like I was just going to die at any moment.

It felt sometimes like all we did at Auburn was run. We'd start out our days with six-minute miles. Then we'd go through all our drills, working out in that hot afternoon sun. All that work would really take it out of you. At the end of the day you'd have to do another six-minute mile. If you didn't make your time, you'd have to keep on running miles until you got it done. Guys would be so gassed at the end of practice, they'd barely crawl to their cars. Sometimes when they got back home to their apartments they wouldn't have the energy to get out of their cars and go inside, so they'd just spend the night sacked out in their vehicles. In the morning they'd shower, clean up and head back out to class.

What with all that running, Auburn baseball practices were physically tougher than any high school football practice I'd ever gone through. Very intense sessions, with guys falling out all the time. People were so intent on getting their miles done inside six minutes they'd push themselves till they dropped in their tracks. Rather die now than have to run this sucker again! One day Mickey Miller fell into the hedges down the right field line. Cramps in both legs, he couldn't get up. He lay in that hedge screaming for help, but we all just ran right past him. Nobody would stop. We hollered out that we'd come back for him in a minute, but we were not going to miss our time. Poor Mick had to lie there until we could finish up, then double back and get him. Those were boot camp conditions, and though we get together and laugh about it now, back then it really seemed like do or die.

How much running did we do at Auburn? At one point I had shin splints so bad I was having to take ten aspirins every day. Empirins they were, a little bit stronger than aspirin. I would take two before practice, two right after practice. Two before I'd go to bed, and I'd wake up in the middle of the night hurting and have to take two more. Then I'd take two when I got up in the morning. Ten a day, and I just could not get rid of that pain. Those shin splints would get to hurting so much by the end of practice that I would have to get a friend to drive me from the ballpark across the parking lot to the clubhouse where we dressed, because it just hurt too much to walk.

Finally one day when we were doing our running, just going on and on around the field as though that dusty circuit were a mill we were doomed to tread forever, I got out into centerfield on about the third or fourth lap and just had to pull up, couldn't run any more for the pain in both my legs. So I slowed up and started walking, kind of hobbling along. Came into home plate, the head coach, Paul Nix, is standing there, getting in my face, calling me a quitter. "What's the matter with you, boy?" There he is hollering at me and I can barely walk. I was going to just walk right past him, but I was so mad I turned around and looked him in the eye. "Listen," I said. "My legs are hurting. I am in some serious pain from all this running. Let's just make a decision here, do you want me to run or do you want me to pitch? Because if you keep running me like this, I'm not going to be able to stand up out on that mound and pitch for you."

Looking back, however, I'll have to say there were two sides to being made to do all that running. When I wasn't hurt from it, I was in pretty good shape. I mean when I was not in pain I could do some serious running. Worked hard at it, and got down to doing about a 5:05 mile. Of course, we had guys who could run a 4:30. Guys who could fly. Every time I was tempted to start getting impressed with myself, one of them would zip right past me. There was a guy named Davis May, who was also a pitcher, we called him the six-million-dollar man, he had just amazing speed. Then we had another fellow named David O'Hare, he'd be right there beside Davis May. And Joe Beckwith, who later played for the Dodgers and Kansas City, he could do a little bit of running too. Those people could get around a baseball field, and being with them made me push myself to get a little better at running, just to try to keep up with them.

The Job

In college practices we used two different types of baseballs. One of them had black print on it, one had blue. They were handed-down National and American League balls, I guess. Well, I could feel the difference between those two kinds of balls. I could tell you which one was the blue one and which the black, without even looking. I could tell by the size. My hands are very small, so any little bit of difference in size and weight in a baseball, I can pick it up immediately. But when I told the coaches I could *feel* the difference in those balls, they wouldn't believe me. And Coach Nix, he put me to the test. He mixed up a couple of balls, one with print of each color, and put one in each of my hands, without my looking. I told him which was which. He tried that test five times in a row. I picked out the correct one every time. Those coaches were amazed. But that's how accustomed I already was to my job, handling baseballs. Any little bit of a difference in a ball will make a difference in how you are going to be able to throw it. Noticing those differences was never any big problem to me; I thought it was a piece of cake, to tell you the truth. It didn't mean too much to me at the time, but later on that little ability of noticing differences would get to be real important to me in this line of work, once I had to learn to get along without my big fastball.

The Cost

I wasn't the only good starting pitcher in my time at Auburn. We always had real good pitching there. Davis May was outstanding. Joe Beckwith, who was a year younger than me, was also very good. Robert Hudson was good. But I think they depended on me a lot, because they knew I was steady. I'd go out there and I'd be able to cover a certain amount of the game for them. I gave them my innings. From being a long reliever in my first few years I'd now become a starter, and in my senior year I just about doubled the number of innings I pitched. Threw six complete games. But I paid the price. Hurt my elbow halfway through the season. After that pitching was never quite the same for me.

My sophomore year, when I went 9-0, I wasn't primarily a starter. They didn't think I was ready yet. But by the time I was a senior, I started games. Got a lot of work. At that time I was throwing everything hard. Ninety-two, ninety-three miles per hour. I would pitch a nine inning game and throw maybe three breaking balls. I didn't really have a breaking ball. If I did try to throw one, it was just to see what would happen. I was lucky if it came within honorable proximity to the strike zone. But it was just for fun. I sure didn't need it. Here I had the gift of a ninety-plus-mile-an-hour fastball. And man, that fastball would explode on people. I'd launch it and it would just take off.

When you're given a gift like that, it's easy to think it will last forever. I didn't ever think to take care of my arm, at that point. I didn't worry about anything like that. And back then there wasn't the knowledge of conditioning you have now, there were no stretches or exercises you did specifically for your arm — at least none that we knew of. So I just went out and kept pouring on the heat, putting a terrific amount of strain on my elbow with every pitch I threw. You can visualize this if you look at the angle I've got my arm in, bent just about to breaking point, in the photo of me throwing a pitch in an Auburn uniform on the cover of this book. It hurts me just to look at the photo, now. So finally I just blew my elbow out. Tore up the ligament. I could feel it snap. The thing healed up on its own after a while so I could pitch again, but I could never again throw as hard. And of course that changed everything.

The way it went down was kind of funny. Toward the end of my senior season, my arm was hurting quite a bit, yet I was throwing extremely well. That's real weird right there. I had that same thing much later on, when I was finishing up my career with the White Sox. At that time, too, my arm was hurting, but I was throwing the ball extremely well. And both times, I tried to push it, to get a little bit more out of it. I ended up hurting myself real bad both times. Both times, I could feel that snap.

I remember we were going to play L. S. U., spring of 1976. It had come down to where we needed to win only a game or two to take the Southwestern Conference championship. We were playing a doubleheader. Joe Beckwith pitched the first game. Joe got beat. I was going to start the second game. I remember my arm was hurting, but I was already used to being in pain when I pitched. I took a couple of Empirins and drank a beer. I said, "All right, now I'm gonna kick it in." Man, I went out and pitched one fantastic baseball game. I used two catchers that night and I think both of them had swollen hands the next day. Because I was just bringing some serious heat that night. A scout who was there told me he'd been clocking pitches. He said I threw as hard as anybody in the country that night.

I won that game for Auburn, and we were SEC champs. That's the high note. But one low note I haven't mentioned yet — the very next game after that, I blew my arm out.

It happened late in the game, along about the sixth or seventh inning. We were playing this little team from Mercer University over in Georgia — over near where Jimmy Carter is from. They had an annual charity game over there, and we'd go in every year and play somebody. We played Georgia Tech one year, and now this other team. When it got into the later innings, I started losing velocity. The hitters, they were getting on me. "Hey, Stud, who stole your smoke?" So I got a little mad and tried to pop one real hard. And the elbow just snapped. Before I even released that pitch my catcher was coming out from behind the plate. He saw my arm give out, I think he might have even heard it. When I got to a certain point in my delivery, my face must have lit up with a flash of pain. My arm went dead, and I just barely threw the ball. Before it even got to him, that catcher was standing up, yelling to the umpire for time out. He called time before the pitch ever got to him. He knew something was seriously wrong. Next thing I knew, he's coming out to me. Then the coaches came out. I said, "Something happened."

Like I said, I'd torn the collateral ligament in my elbow. I know that now, but nobody knew that then. That feeling — back then we didn't know what it was.

It snapped. I could feel it. And I said to myself at that moment, there goes that. That was not meant to be. But things happen for a reason.

So that was the end of me pitching, basically, for a while. I was out. I tried to rest and come back. There was a period of time when I could barely throw a ball from the pitcher's mound to home plate.

The main course of healing that was recommended to me was to go running. I did a lot of running, trying to get the blood-flow going in my elbow. They wanted to get me back in there as soon as possible. The arm healed back up enough so that I ended up pitching again at the end of the year. As I said, that season we went to the Southern Regional playoffs. I think they were trying to get around having to pitch me, because I was hurting. But that was pressure time, and so they decided to start me against Florida State in the Southern Regional semifinal game. I went about seven innings in that game, and actually did very well. So as to protect my elbow, I changed the angle of my arm and worked from overhead just a little bit more in that game. But there was a cost. Changing my delivery like that, I injured something in my shoulder. So now, out of that game I came, with my elbow feeling better, but a brand new pain in my shoulder.

I forgot to mention that at the time I had to come out of the Florida State game, I had a shutout going. In fact I was dominating in that game. I wasn't throwing quite as hard as I had earlier, but I was nice and smooth. I remember when I went out to get ready for that game, I warmed up for forty-five minutes. Practically pitched a whole game before the game even started, I was that concerned. Just to make sure everything was flowing again. Well, we won that game, which gave us a chance to go on in the playoffs. We went on and won our next game, too, won the Southern Regionals and went on to the World Series. I was hurting and couldn't pitch much more that season, though. It took me a while to get over the damage I'd done to my shoulder.

Part Three

Out on the
Roads of Life

The Biggest Waste of Time I Ever Saw

When I got through playing baseball at college, I didn't really know what I wanted to do with my life. I was still some credits shy of my degree from Auburn. Playing baseball was the one thing I was qualified to do, but I had never really thought that much about doing it professionally. At Auburn we were all looking forward in some hopeful way to getting drafted, of course. I was still thinking that way, even after hurting my pitching arm my senior year. I just thought I needed some rest, and my arm would heal back up. I had a feeling that I could still play ball a little bit, for somebody. I thought Double-A ball might be the highest level I could go, but I still wanted to see if I could get that far or possibly even higher. The trouble was, it seemed nobody wanted to pick up a pitcher with a bad arm. To make matters worse, I was a little bit overweight at this time. As I've said, I always did enjoy eating. From coming into college at 185 pounds, by now I was probably up to about 215. I wasn't looking that good to the scouts. But even if I didn't have too many people interested in me as a prospect, I was not about to quit without giving it a shot.

A little while after school let out I heard Cincinnati was holding a tryout camp over in Albany, Georgia. The camp was due to start at ten o'clock. I got up at four o'clock in the morning to drive over there. Wanted to make sure I was on time. Got there about nine o'clock, but nobody had told me where the field was. Drove around a while till somehow or other I found a baseball field, which just happened to be the right one. There must have been 250 other guys there, representing just about every different stage of baseball skill and baseball getup you could imagine, all looking for a contract. The scouts over there timed us running, watched us throwing a little bit, then started up a little inter-squad game in which everybody was going to get to show what they could do. It was my first time back pitching since I'd hurt my arm. I threw one inning, struck out all three hitters. My arm definitely wasn't right, but I was still throwing pretty good. They gave me a little pat on the back and said, "Thanks for coming, see you later. We don't really need anybody right now." I said, "Well, then, why the heck are you holding this tryout?" I drove four hours to get over here, and didn't get paid one cent for my trouble. I didn't have any money at the time. I was plenty disappointed. I go over here thinking I'm going to impress somebody, and it seems like they were never interested. They said, "We'll keep you in mind."

That Cincinnati tryout was the biggest waste of time I ever saw. The only thing I got out of it was a little bit of a message. Here I thought I'd gotten myself somewhere in baseball, but now I saw I was just starting out on what was going to be a long road.

Baton Rouge, Louisiana

As I say, my friend Mickey hadn't been drafted either. At one point we'd been told Cincinnati intended to pick us up, even though they didn't draft us. No matter, they were just going to go ahead and sign us. But they didn't do it. So we had nowhere to go. But now what we did was go out and play for the Baton Rouge Cougars, a Single-A team in the independent Gulf States League. It was a professional league, but the teams had no affiliation to any major league team. Mickey came up with the idea somehow or other. They asked us to come out and play, and oh have mercy, all of a sudden we thought we were the finest thing that ever walked around. Because now we were going to get paid three hundred and fifty dollars a month to play baseball. We thought we were rich. Oh, we were just in heaven. We were going to get to meet some new people, and get paid some big-time money!

Mick and I lit out for Baton Rouge in my beat-up Datsun with the broken driver's seat. I had these two logs propped behind my seat, to hold it up so I could drive. We were really going to be seeing the South in style. We rolled out of Selma with a load of clothes, our baseball gear and a couple of roast beef sandwiches contributed by Mickey's mom. I mean, we just took off driving, heading for Baton Rouge. We didn't know what route to take to get there or even who to look up when we arrived. We didn't know what to expect, but it was an adventure, and we were definitely primed.

When we finally drove into town and located the hotel we were supposed to stay at, they told us the Baton Rouge Cougars weren't there. The season was already going on, and the team was out on the road. But then the manager of the team called in to say somebody had got hurt, he needed a player right then. So they flew Mickey out to join them. That left me hanging out back there in the hotel on my lonesome. The one other Cougars player who was there was a guy named Sterling Allen, so I hung around a little bit with him. He had played up at a somewhat higher level of ball, maybe Double-A. This guy could run, I mean, man, he could fly: I saw that when we worked out together over at the baseball park at L. S. U., where the Cougars played. Being able to run well sure wasn't getting Sterling wealthy in baseball, though. Next to him, I was a rich man, since I was still getting some support from my mom and dad. So I'd take him out for beers and pizza. I was doing a lot more eating than pitching and throwing, at that point. For a fat kid, I really needed to be doing a lot more work than I was doing.

Then the Cougars came into town. It looked like they had a pretty good team, and they were winning. When I joined the team, they had only nine games left in the first half of the Gulf States League season, and they were in first place. They had some outstanding players. There was one guy, Tom Brown, who signed up with Seattle and had a short stint in the big leagues, then eventually became a pitching coach for the Orioles, I believe. There were some other players who were pretty good. I doubt you've ever heard of them, but they could play. Myself, I pitched mostly in relief at Baton Rouge. I started one game, and I finished it. But my arm was still hurting a lot of the time. I wasn't throwing the ball anywhere near as well as I had been in college, and being way overweight sure wasn't helping.

But for a while, Mickey and I were enjoying the life. We were playing ball and having ourselves a pretty good time. We took an apartment with two other guys on the team. Four of us living in a little three-bedroom apartment right off the L. S. U. campus. Well, we were trying to save money. Those roommates we had were not my favorite guys on that team, though. I just didn't care for them. Most of the players down there were great guys, and we got along just fine. But there's always somebody in every team who's got just a little different opinion of themselves, how things ought to go and how everybody ought to treat them. That apartment could get to feeling a little close. And Lord, it was smoking hot down there in Baton Rouge in the middle of the summer. We lived on a street called Alaska Drive, which I could never figure out. Alaska? How did they ever come up with that name, in a steambath like that?

Well, we were going to have a good time anyway. If we wanted cool, we could create our own. We kept that air-conditioning cranked all the way up at all times. Ice cold inside that apartment, at any hour. Sleep till ten, then get up and check out the Gong Show. That was the happening game show on the tube at that time. Then Mickey and I would go out and get lunch. We just loved a place called Picadilly Cafeteria. Man, they had the finest seafood gumbo, with all the vegetables and everything. Now with me thinking I had money coming in, I was eating better and better, and really ballooning up. In fact, what with all that eating and not getting to pitch too much because of my arm still hurting (only nineteen innings all summer), by the time I got out of Baton Rouge I'd pumped up close to 225. Oh, I could still get around on the field. I could still run. It would surprise people how quick I could move. But boy, was I a fat pig. I knew that some day I was going to have to lose it all. I was some kind of ugly. I had the ugliest Fu Manchu goatee deal you ever saw in your life. I figured if I was going to be fat I might just as well be ugly to go along with it.

In the second half of the season we went out and ran off with that league. We were out in front by seven games with only fourteen games left. Then the team folded. The owner ran out of cash and couldn't meet the payroll, and the Baton Rouge Cougars went belly up with two weeks still left in the Gulf States League season. When they informed us the team was bankrupt we were all the way down in Harlingen, Texas, just a stone's throw from Mexico. At this time the team was traveling in a couple of borrowed Kindercare vans. So here we were, twenty sweaty, exhausted baseball players in kindergarten vans with no money. We had to sneak out of the hotel in Harlingen. I believe we had the police out looking for us.

We hightailed it in those kiddie vans all the way back to Baton Rouge. The league directed us to stop in Corpus Christi, where our next scheduled game was supposed to be played. Now, we hadn't been paid in a month. We said, no way are we going to stop to play that game in Corpus Christi. So we headed straight for Baton Rouge, drove all across East Texas like a bunch of bank robbers on the run and made the trip in one long nasty day. When we got back there, everybody but a few married guys had given up their apartments. There was just one unmarried guy who'd kept his. We had fifteen or sixteen guys sleeping on the floor in that guy's place. The league got the guy's number and the next thing we know, the league president is on the phone, ordering us to turn around and head back to Corpus Christi to play that game. If we didn't do it, he told us, none of us would ever play professional baseball again in our lives. Well, at this point, Mickey and I couldn't have cared less. We decided we weren't going back to Corpus Christi no matter what that league told us. We just put the whole thing on hold, and that was the end of our big fling with the Baton Rouge Cougars.

We did have a blast while we were down there. Met some good people. It's too bad things got shut down the way they did. We didn't end up getting blacklisted by professional baseball, though. I think everybody could understand how a man would not want to go on playing in an independent league when he wasn't getting paid. I think that league only lasted about three more years before it folded up altogether.

But I feel pretty privileged to have gotten a chance to play anywhere at all at that point. And it was a real experience. One or two times when we didn't have those Kindercare vans to travel in, some of the guys would drive their cars. One of the other guys from Alabama on the team, a kid from Birmingham, had this big old Chevrolet Caprice convertible, baby blue, with a white top. And boy, we'd pop that old top down and we'd hit the road, cruising all the way down into Texas in that beautiful big convertible. What a sight we thought we were — the hottest thing on wheels, showboating through Houston and all the way on down. Oh, we had just a wonderful time. Victoria, Texas. Beeville, Texas. Harlingen. Corpus Christi. Man we hit some high life, it was big time. That summer we thought we were what everybody in the world was waiting to see.

Would You Like to Sign a Contract?

After the independent league team dissolved in Baton Rouge, I went on back to school. I still needed to finish up a couple of quarters for my degree, and I got in one of those quarters that fall. When it came around to spring of '77, I left school again and went back home to Selma. I played softball all I could, all through that time. I would play on two different teams, a church league team and a commercial league team. Play a couple times a week with each team, then if one was playing in a tournament on the weekend I'd go with them. If there came a weekend when neither one of those teams was playing, I'd find some other team that needed a player for a tournament somewhere. Always made sure I was playing in a softball game somewhere at least four or five times a week.

Right away, I started losing a little weight. I was still heavy, but now I was getting down to 210, 205. And I was really making an effort to strengthen my arm back up. Playing all that softball at that point definitely helped me start getting it back in shape. I'd play outfield, where I could do a lot of long throwing and get my mechanics back and get a little power back in my arm. I never got it all back but I got some. I played no baseball at that time, only slow pitch softball. I did not even throw a baseball. Throwing a softball around allowed me to build up arm strength without putting too much of a strain on it. Around home I would throw against walls. Put up tape in a little square on the wall, and try to hit it. Working on control there. My father and mother were always behind me. They still had faith in my ability to play baseball. They still believed I could get somewhere.

And then, come to find out they were right. I got a tryout with the Braves up in Atlanta, and they signed me to my first real contract.

Now earlier I'd been to a few other tryouts like that Cincinnati affair I mentioned. I was not impressed, they were not impressed with me. Those were just mob scenes, mostly. But this Atlanta tryout was a special deal, by invitation only. We had a friend of the family who was a scout, Julian Mock, and Mr. Mock helped me get in on this. My father drove over to Atlanta stadium with me. I think there were only 29 people at this tryout, as opposed to hundreds. There were nine pitchers on hand, everybody was going to get a turn to throw. But I was way down on the list — next-to-last man. That was not a good sign. My dad and I were sitting over in the hotel next door to the stadium, waiting for my turn. At that point, I wasn't feeling too good about my chances. I was figuring this was just going to be the same thing as before, only fewer people — another big waste of time. I was just about ready to pack up my gear and get out of there, in fact. But then it hit me how much trouble my dad had gone to, helping me set this up. "All right," I said, "I'm just going to hang out here and throw and see what happens."

Finally my turn came up. Like I've said, I no longer could throw as hard as I used to. Where once I was regularly getting my fastball up there at ninety-two, ninety-three miles per hour, now, after messing up my elbow and shoulder, I might have been able to push it into the high eighties, but that was without any of the serious movement or explosion on my pitches that I used to have. I had just basic mediocre stuff now, but I was still out there busting my butt to hump it up there as hard as I could. And that was not going to do it. Something extra was going to have to be brought to bear. Here I am at the point of giving up this whole big league dream, without too much hope of anything. At times like that you don't have anything to lose. You make up pitches as you need them. You do what you have to do to survive. So that day I threw sliders, changeups, you name it — pitches I'd never thrown in my life. Somehow or other that day I came up with those pitches, pretty much out of desperation I suppose. I started out with fastballs, getting it up to 88, 89. I didn't really have a slider, but I threw a kind of hard curve, at like 85, 86, and the scouts thought that was a slider. I'd be thinking I was throwing a curve, you know, and because I was throwing it as hard as I could, they'd be thinking it was a slider. They thought that was pretty good. And then, I'd never had a changeup either, but that day I dropped a change-up on a guy. I kind of slowed everything up and just lobbed it up there. Dang, it looked good! The guy was a big left-handed batter. He swung so hard he like to screwed himself into the ground, and missed that pitch big-time. I couldn't help getting a little chuckle out of that. I was feeling better now. And then what I did next really impressed those scouts most of all, I think. The same hitter was standing back in there, really digging in to get after me now. And I just reared back and threw the hardest fastball I could throw. It nailed that poor dude right in the neck. He kind of did the tuna on the ground, thrashing around in the dirt there for a little bit. Now I didn't feel too good about that. But I'm standing out there anyway with this look on my face that says, "You're going to be taking your life in your hands if you ever again try to dig in on me like that."

That little bit of wildness was no problem for those scouts, since on all my other pitches I'd shown pretty decent control. I was just wild enough to be effective, as the saying goes. Well, the next thing I did was start walking off the field. I wasn't more than ten steps off the mound when the director of the tryout called over to me, "Hey, would you like to sign a contract?" It actually happened like that, while I was still walking off the field. It was an easy question to answer. Well, what else did they think I was there for?

I said, Heck, yeah, I sure did mean to sign. They told me they wanted me to go down to Greenwood, South Carolina, and pitch for the Braves' Single-A team there. "How soon can you be there?" "Oh, no problem, I can take off right now, be there in the morning!" Man, I was fired up. They said, "No, take a little time, report in three days." I said, "You got it, I'll be there."

I went in and cleaned up and went back over to the ballpark to sign a contract. This was definitely a big event for me, I was up in the big offices of a major league club signing a real contract. They're going to give me five hundred dollars a month to play baseball. I'd been in Baton Rouge making three fifty. That's a hundred and fifty dollar a month raise. Signing that first contract I was so excited I actually mispelled my own name. Put only one "R" in my first name. My hand just didn't seem to be able to calm down long enough to write that second R. I was secretly worried somebody might notice, but nobody even said anything about it. For my signing bonus they gave me an apple and a road map to get to Greenwood, South Carolina. Well, they did also pick up my hotel bill and my lunch tab on the way home. I sure wasn't about to ask for more.

That trip turned out to be one wonderful experience for me. When I signed the contract, my dad and I felt so pleased we almost didn't know what to say. On the way back home we stopped off in Auburn and I saw a couple of old buddies of mine. Told them I'd gone to this tryout and got myself signed. It was awesome news to everybody. My friends and I were just jumping around like kids. What a day. Drove on back to Selma, and ended up celebrating in a roadhouse outside town half the night. Everybody I knew in my home town was happy for me.

Greenwood, South Carolina

Once I got my celebrating done I had another day or two to hang around Selma before reporting to the Atlanta farm team. Maybe my three days' grace time was too long after all, because while I was back home I like to ruined my career before I'd even got it started. Went down to the Alabama River to do a little water skiing, a real brilliant plan. Everything went fine until I tried to jump the wake of the boat and get some hang time. That water came up on me way too fast. I did the splits when I hit and felt something tweak in my groin. Pulled a muscle right there. I limped back home, couldn't really walk much less run. You can bet I was one worried puppy at that point. Luckily I could move around a little better when I woke up in the morning. So I counted my blessings, threw my gear in my car and set out to find my way to Greenwood, South Carolina.

I found out there were certain adjustments I was going to have to make right away, at this new level of professional baseball. First off, when the Braves assigned me to Greenwood they told me to look up Kenny Rowe, the pitching coach. Well, at Auburn, you were kind of deferential, you called your coaches "Coach." Back there, when you talked to Dennis Womack, who was one of the assistant coaches, it was "Coach Womack," not "Dennis." That's what I was used to. But now when I get to the ballpark and get ahold of Kenny Rowe, the first thing I do is drop a "Coach Rowe" on him, and everybody busts out laughing. Calling a coach "Coach" turns out to be the dumbest rookie mistake you can make, over here in professional baseball. Over here, you're just supposed to be calling him "Kenny." The other players were all getting on me about that, and then I couldn't figure out half of what they were saying. At least half that team was Latin, and they were talking Spanish. I didn't know two words of Spanish. Here was another thing I was going to have to pick up on. Well, this was all quite an experience for me. It was new, but yet it was pretty exciting at the same time.

I got in late. Found my hotel, spent the night. In the morning we took off on a road trip. There came my next shock. In college we'd had these nice big Greyhound buses to ride around in. Well, I might not have thought they were so nice and big at the time, but now they were looking a whole lot more comfortable in hindsight. Because here at Greenwood what they packed you into was an ancient yellow school bus. No air-conditioning, hard metal seat-backs, everybody doubled up two to a seat with knees jammed nearly up to your chin. Crammed into this rickety old bus, I'm getting to know my new teammates for the first time as we wait to get going. I'm real apprehensive about everything, not to mention a little bit homesick. In Baton Rouge I'd had my friend Mickey with me, here I was definitely on my own. Everybody around me's talking Spanish. Those guys weren't too much longer out of their home towns than I was out of mine. They couldn't understand me and I couldn't understand them. I'm saying to myself, "Oh, Lord, what have I got myself into now?" I had no idea. Right at that moment, I was giving very little thought to my big league prospects. The only thing I could think about was getting back off that bus and going home.

Then some more guys got on the bus. Fortunately for me, a couple of them could speak English. Stu Livingstone, Mike Reynolds, Mike Paciorek. Mike's brother Tom Paciorek I later played with in New York and then he ended up as the White Sox announcer. Those two guys looked and talked almost identical, Mike and Tom, and both were great guys. but the point right here was I finally had somebody I could talk to, and that helped me out a lot.

I got friendly with all three of those guys, and when we got back from that first road trip they let me move in with them in this house they were sharing. Little brick factory row-house, built for milltown textile workers. A heat wave hit about the time I got there. It was like 110, 112 degrees every day, the first two or three weeks I spent in Greenwood, South Carolina. It just stayed hot. Hottest place I've ever been. And we had one dinky fan, and no air-conditioning. The house totally lacked air circulation, it was just a little square pile of bricks soaking up the heat and sucking it in.

You'd come back home after playing a game, you'd be extremely hot and sweaty. The dressing room out at the ballpark was the smallest dressing room I ever saw. It was so crowded in there I once saw a guy changing out of his uniform put his foot into the leg of somebody else's underwear. Most guys would just grab enough clothes to cover up and then rush right outside into the night air to cool themselves off. We'd jump into our cars and run out to the Wooden Door, this little old country bar we liked. They had ice cold beer on draft there, and they'd let us sing and carry on. Two a.m., they'd throw us out and we'd have to go back to that little old brick house. The thermometer would say ninety-nine degrees inside, and man those bricks were just radiating heat. You were inside an oven. We did what we could to get a little sleep, but it was pretty near impossible.

Stu liked to sleep in the nude. He was always lying around naked. I couldn't go quite that far. These were people I didn't know, I'd never been living in this type of situation before. We'd soak towels in cold water and lay the towels across our chests and lie there. We'd turn on that fan, and aim it around different ways, trying to get a little breeze going. We'd go out in my car and crank the air-conditioning way up and just sit there for a while. We'd drive over to the 7-11 and grab a coke and we'd drive on back. Nothing worked, you just didn't sleep all night. It was miserable.

The one guy who ever managed to catch any little stretch of shuteye in that hothouse was Mike Reynolds. Rennie, he was a piece of work. Loved to play the game of baseball, real hard core. We called him Taz, because he was just like the Tasmanian Devil. We'd come in at night sometimes, and Mike would be laid out in the middle of that furnace, dead to the world. He was *hard*. Did everything hard, even *slept* hard. The rest of us were always looking to run off to somewhere cooler. Now we knew Mike wouldn't want to get left out. So we'd have to slap him around to get him up. We'd say, "Hey, we're going to go out here and meet some people for a while" — it'd be twelve, one o'clock in the morning — "you want to go?" And he'd just snap right up and say, "Man, I was born ready." He'd be up, out of the bed, ready to go. I never did understand how he could do it — especially the way he got ready. He'd pull his blue jeans on, then he'd put on his boots. No socks. No socks at all, just put his boots on and go. And I'd say, "Man, I've got to have socks on with my boots."

Before long all four of us were wearing out real early in the ballgames at night, because we just never slept at all. Finally it got too hot even for Mike to sleep. We went on like that for a couple of weeks, then we just couldn't stand it any more. We tried hanging out as much as we could in any air-conditioned buildings we could find, but of course they always kicked you out at night. In the end we all split up and went off with other players into air-conditioned apartments or trailers, where we could finally get some sleep at night.

I moved into a trailer out on a lake outside Greenwood with Wyatt Tonkin from Seattle, who was a great guy and a lot of fun to be with, and Larry Owen, a new kid who had come in after me. I'd arrived at Greenwood about two weeks before the halfway break in the season, and Larry had come in just at the break, so my being two weeks up on him made me like a veteran to him. That little household accepted me right away. Right off Larry and I were laughing and cutting up like kids who had grown up together. We all three got along great. It was a little cooler out by the lake, or we thought it was. The air-conditioning system in the trailer only worked in the living room, so those two guys sacked out on mattresses on the living room floor while I laid out on the couch. That way we were able to get a little bit of sleep out there. The summer at Greenwood ended up with everybody draped out over floors and couches, gasping for a cool breeze.

A New Delivery

The funny thing is, that sweltering '77 season actually turned my career right around. During that smoking Carolina summer the Greenwood pitching coach, Kenny Rowe, helped me come up with a brand new sidearm delivery that gave me a new movement on my pitches and a new lease on my baseball life.

The change came real quick, once it came. They didn't pitch me at all at Greenwood, my first two weeks. They just kept an eye on me while I got my arm in shape. Kenny Rowe watched me. I was still throwing overhand, like I had in the tryout camp. I was now getting some arm strength back. I still didn't have a breaking ball, but I'd developed a slider. I was throwing overhand okay, with a little bit of movement. But Kenny had another idea, he wanted to see more. "Have you ever tried this?" And he dropped down and showed me a kind of sidearm whipping motion. Well, now and then I'd tried throwing the ball sidearm just playing around, but I had never worked at it seriously. Now when I tried to throw it with Kenny, right away I was surprised at the movement I got. My pitches from down under had very good movement. So we kept working on it. I got into the last game before the halfway break, and then in the second half of the season Greenwood started using me pretty regularly in relief. There were 71 games I was eligible for, and I got in 20 games and threw 67 innings. That was the most I'd thrown in quite a while, and a lot of those times I was really in a zone out there on the mound.

With my new way of coming at the hitters from down under, pitching for me suddenly stopped being a matter of blowing people out with my power and became a matter of finessing with my movement. When I'd thrown overhand and hard I'd had to beat people up, overpower them. Now I adopted a completely different approach. It took more courage than anything I'd ever tried in pitching. That's because of the speed I was throwing at, which was primarily slow. You have to have guts to throw the ball as slow as I was consistently throwing it, with that new sidearm motion. When you throw hard, you feel dominant on the mound. For a while, after I'd lost that dominating speed, I'd been at the hitter's mercy. Now, once I got that new delivery going and learned how I could really get the ball to move and how to place it, I could turn the situation back around. I could take control again.

I was a whole new pitcher. I'd never been much of a strikeout guy, but now, though I was only throwing in the mid-eighties at best, ten miles per hour below my onetime prime, I was using that new little Laredo slider from south of the border to strike people out all over the place: 67 strikeouts in 67 innings, by far the best ratio I'd ever had. I had such success with that new delivery, I came into games and struck out the side a number of times. A lot of those hitters I struck out on three pitches. It was unbelievable how far those guys were missing the ball. I could not believe my eyes. They would miss it by a foot and a half. My catcher would jump out to take the pitch, and the guy would still be swinging at it. I really had it working. And on top of that, now here comes a nice little sinker. And then, what with my arm getting stronger, my fastball starts to pick up a little hop. Guys who are not striking out against me are hitting feeble little groundballs. I felt lucky, it was an embarrassment of riches. I'd hit on a real nice mix of sidearm with overhand pitches, and from then on I just stuck with that formula. It *worked*. I never messed with any other pitches until I got to the major leagues.

I wasn't thinking out that far ahead of myself yet. My object for the time being was still getting to Double-A. But I was definitely thankful for the way things had gone with my season. To some degree the Atlanta organization must have felt that way too. At the end of the year they asked me back.

Part Four
What it Takes
to Survive

Off-Season

I knew one nice year in Single-A ball wasn't enough to guarantee me a career in baseball, so when that season at Greenwood was over I went back to college and finished up my degree. That winter I graduated from Auburn with a bachelor's degree in Personal Management / Industrial Relations. I'd never been a great student and it had taken me quite a bit of effort to stay after that degree and finally get it, so I felt real proud. What had kept me going on it was saying to myself, "Hey, you just might need this later on." And ever since then when I've talked with young kids just coming up in baseball, I've always told them no matter how much bonus money they get they ought to make sure they take care of their education. You never know what might happen. The next time you step out on that mound you might blow out your arm, but if you've got that education, you can always figure out some other way to make a living.

Between the end of school and the start of spring training I went home to Selma. From that year on, I'd always pick up some little job back home when baseball wasn't going on. I wasn't exactly getting rich as a ballplayer in the minor leagues. I was making between five and six hundred dollars a month, my first few years in the minors, and those monthly checks came in only during the summers. That's five checks a year. I didn't get paid anything at all in spring training, and I didn't get paid anything in the winter. If I was making $500 a month, my annual baseball salary came to $2500. That won't support you very long.

Fortunately I knew people in Selma who'd help me out with off-season jobs. My first couple of years in the minors I worked on and off during the winters at Minit shops, which are like 7-11 type convenience stores. They taught me how to work the cash register, how to total up, how to do inventories. I'd mop the floors and clean up at closing time, then run over and put the money in the bank. Whatever else needed to be done, I'd just figure out a way and then go ahead and do it. I worked the late shift, till eleven o'clock, and they liked having a man there to do that, because they thought standing alone at a convenience store cash register at night was not a job for a lady.

Other times I worked for some people who owned a chain of gas stations, the Cougar Gas Company it was called. They hired me to run this no-account little station over on Selma Avenue. "Manager" was my official title, but the office was just a glass box. Inside they had a cash register, some cans of oil, some cigarettes and a few coolers full of beer. Outside, two sets of gas pumps, self-service at one island and at the other I'd do the honors. Now Selma can get cold in the middle of winter. I'd come in at six o'clock in the morning to open up and the temperature would be like sixteen degrees. Pretty nippy for pumping gas.

To tell you the truth, nobody else wanted that job, so I wound up working a whole lot of overtime hours there in the winters. I needed the money and I liked being out there on my own, but oh my, that place could get cold. All I had for heat inside my "office" was two little space heaters. I'd have those suckers fired up going as hard as they could. A lot of days it would be wet, too. There'd be women going to work in the morning who'd stop in there for gas and not want to get out and pump it for themselves, so they'd pull up to the full-service island and I'd have to run on out. It's wet out there, and freezing cold. I get out there and they want two dollars' worth of gas. "That'll be all, thank you very much." Pumping that two dollars' worth of gas would be enough to get my clothes soaked through for the rest of the day. I'd be huddled in that little glass cubicle with my teeth chattering, trying my best to get warm.

But then all those overtime hours did provide me any spare money I was going to have. I drove a bigger car by this time, and that big boat was guzzling up some gas. Remember we're talking about 1978, now, gas is getting pretty expensive. I'd take it real easy so as to get through the week on a half tank, which was about ten dollars' worth. Running on fumes by the end of every week, but at least I'd be sticking to my budget. I was always tucking away a little something from every paycheck I got. By the end of the winter I'd be able to have enough of a lump saved up so that when I got to spring training and one of the other guys was running short, I could help him out. Or if there was an apartment deposit to make, I'd be the guy who could put that down. It was a real good habit to get into, I always thought, saving my money like that. Of course I'll admit that what really made my whole little economy possible, in those years, was the good luck I had in being able to live at home. Mom and dad fed me real good and if something came up that I needed, they'd always be there to help me out.

But I really wanted to be independent and on my own, at this time. I liked living in my home town but I looked forward to a day when I could get my own place; I wasn't quite there yet. I was single and I was young. I had some wild and crazy friends I did my share of goofing off with. Some real good friends, several of them. After work we'd run around town to the different night clubs, hanging out, laughing and cutting up. It didn't make any difference to us if we had girls with us or not. If we were just stuck with ourselves, that was all right with us. We thought we were the hottest thing around. We didn't care what happened as long as we had a beer in our hands. If you just let us laugh and sing and carry on, we had no problems in the world.

Spring Training (1978)

So here I am in West Palm Beach, Florida, at my first spring training, with the Braves. You've got players from all over the place. Double-A, Triple-A, rookie leagues. When I first looked around, I didn't know anybody. I could have very easily run into a bunch of bad guys. But then instead I ran into a few people I knew from that Single-A team at Greenwood — Mike Reynolds, Stu Livingstone, Larry Owen. Those were guys I'd lived with in that milltown house and in that trailer. We had already been through a little bit together. They were guys pretty much just like me. They were all minor league guys. None of them were very high draft picks. They were just ordinary people, all of them very honest, and they all had big hearts, all they wanted was just to play and to be trying their best.

We had a good time trying together, that spring. We all kind of meshed in. There's a special bond that happens between people when they're all trying to break in together. I still keep in touch with several of those guys to this day. I was real fortunate to have them there, that spring. They kept me going because they were so loose and easy. All together we had ourselves a real trip. In fact after going up from Single-A to Double-A together we all came back to spring training the next year too, and had another blast. By then it was like we'd known each other our whole lives.

Savannah

Larry Owen and myself, we were very much alike. In those days if you saw one of us, you saw the other, because we were always together. I guess we must have had a lot in common, because we never got tired of hanging out. Larry was a catcher. Later he made it to the big leagues with Atlanta and Kansas City, but back then he had no idea what to expect out of life, just like me. We'd had a good time together the prevous year in that trailer over at Greenwood, so now when we both got assigned to the Braves' Double-A team in Savannah, Georgia, we decided we'd try to be roommates again. Larry, myself, and a guy named Jimmy Weissinger set out to find a place to live.

We'd been sent over to Savannah a little bit late in spring training; by the time we got there all the other guys we knew already had apartments that were full. Everything was expensive over there, we found out, and we weren't making much money. At this time my salary might have been moving up to about six hundred dollars a month, Larry must have been making about the same thing, Jimmy might have been making a little bit more but it still didn't look like much once you pooled all our resources together. We were having a very, very hard time finding an apartment. We were so discouraged at one point, we even went out to look at trailers. The one trailer we could afford in Savannah was just the raggediest-looking little thing you had ever seen. A self-respecting rat wouldn't live in it.

A day came when we were all contemplating quitting baseball because we couldn't find anywhere to live. It was that tough, and we were just that discouraged about it. Right then we caught a break. A local man who enjoyed baseball and supported the team let us have an apartment at a rental complex he owned. Very nice apartment, too — solved all our housing problems. But I have to believe it was the last time that man ever did that kind of a favor for a ballplayer, because not too long after moving in, we all got shipped out. We had people taking our place, but then a couple of those people started getting shipped in and out also. I don't think the same person ever stayed in that apartment for over six weeks at any time in that summer. Of course things went from bad to worse. The owner never knew who was living in his place. I can't imagine what that apartment looked like when it was all over — a cyclone would probably make a better tenant than a rotating gang of ballplayers. I always meant to call that man back and apologize and thank him for his generosity, but I never did get to. We owed him a lot, because he got us out of a tough spot. I don't think you can relax and have a good time playing the game of baseball if half your mind is off worrying about where you're going to be putting your head down at night.

On the Bus

When I think of Savannah, Georgia, and playing Double-A with the Braves, the thing I always remember is the long bus rides at night. We made real long trips down there, sometimes we were on that bus twelve hours at a time. Man, those rides sometimes seemed like they were going on *forever*.

I remember once we were traveling between Memphis and Montgomery. At about three or four o'clock in the morning our bus had a flat on a two-lane road about twenty miles outside of Columbus, Mississippi. We asked for help at a farmer's house. It was unbelievable. That farmer got up, wrestled our tire off, drove on into Columbus, woke up a mechanic, got the tire fixed, drove on back and put that tire back on our bus for us. While he was gone his wife made coffee and sandwiches for our whole team. The farmer's whole family was up by now. His young kids kept us entertained. Those boys did knife tricks for us and showed us how to play mumbly-peg. Just great people, rescuing a busload of strangers in the middle of the night.

On those long junkets I'd be a kind of den-mother for the whole team. I'd pack up a big cooler with bologna and stuff to make sandwiches, and everybody would eat out of there. I'd have a six pack of beer in there, cokes, some water. Twelve hours on a bus, people do get thirsty. Then there was the little matter of sleep. I always had a hard time sleeping in those bus seats, they were extremely uncomfortable. You had to feel sorry for the guys who were really tall. We had a real nice fellow named Rich Weeders who was very tall and bony. He was about six feet six. His knees just would not fold up into one of those seats. Any time I was unable to sleep and looking around the bus, he was always sitting there wide awake too.

Some of the guys would attempt to get their rest in various creative ways. There were certain guys who tried to sleep stretched out in the overhead luggage racks. With that method, though, you ran the risk of getting pitched out into the aisle if the bus made a sharp turn or went over a hole in the road. With some of the roads and drivers we had, that was known to happen.

One of my own tricks was to sleep on the aisle-floor on an inflated plastic raft, the kind you put up in your back yard for the kids. I'd bring it on with me and blow it up on board. Of course, lying in the aisle like that you always stood the chance of someone coming along and stepping right on your head. There were nights when even having your skull crunched seemed a small price to pay for a few hours of shuteye. Another slight drawback was having the engines right underneath you. The heat would radiate up and you'd get into a pretty good sweat there on the floor.

A better device I finally came up with for sleeping on buses was a kind of fishnet hammock with ropes on both ends. I'd tie that thing catty-cornered from the baggage compartments at the top of the bus, dangling out there across the walkway. Oh my goodness, that worked nice. No matter how rough the ride got, I would be just floating and swaying along. I had all sorts of people offering to buy that thing from me, but I turned everybody down. It was definitely the best piece of sleeping equipment I ever had on the bus.

It was not easy passing the time on bus rides. After all, you were with the same people night after night, and there weren't many available diversions. We developed a whole lot of different ways to amuse ourselves, though. Of course we drank and cut up and told stories. Everybody came from all different parts of the country. Their different accents and the stories they told about the places they came from made everything interesting. You were always learning something. My friend Stu Livingstone could take a very boring, mundane story and spice it up just by the way he told it. He had one about being at Yellowstone with his wife, trying to take pictures of this bear and the bear coming after them and all. It was a story you might have heard a dozen times before from other people, but the way Stu would get into all the different details, he'd be cracking me up. Everybody would talk about everything they'd ever done, people they'd known, trips they'd taken, places they'd been. We'd tell our stories, and we'd all laugh. We'd tell every joke we'd ever heard. Everybody would manage to find them funny.

The biggest thing we'd do to make the time go by on bus rides was to sing. Three or four of us would take harmony parts and do our renditions of selected golden oldies. We had a little group. Got to be pretty good, too, though we probably never could carry a tune. We knew most of the words and we could make it interesting and get everybody having fun. Guys would be clapping and carrying on to the point where you'd almost forgotten you were locked up in a rolling sweatbox.

Golden Oldies

We liked to sing when we were off the bus, too. I was at Savannah for parts of three seasons, '78 to '80, and my last year there we all moved into this duplex apartment on Wilmington Island, just outside of Savannah, in between Savannah and Savannah Beach. It was just a perfect place, halfway between the beach and the ballpark. Mike and Stu were living out there too — we had both sides of that duplex, it was great. Six of us living out there now, and on Sunday afternoons we'd invite the whole team out for a barbecue. I'd get two or three grills of chicken or steaks going, and we'd have all sorts of little side dishes that the other players' wives would bring around. Sooner or later we'd inevitably get to harmonizing. Even the ladies would want to get on up and join in. Some of those girls who knew the words would sing along, the rest would just hang back there clanging their beer cans and chanting, having fun. The time just flew by. Sometimes I'll hear one of those golden oldie tunes now and it'll make me drift back to those long sweet Savannah Sunday afternoons.

Stu Livingstone would always know the words to every song. Or if he didn't know them all, he could sure come close. We had a game called "Stump Stu," the object of which was to find songs Stu didn't know the words to. We couldn't find anybody that was able to stump him really. Well, at one point I actually came up with a song he had never heard of, and that one got him — but I don't think that ever happened a second time. It was near impossible to find a song that could stump Stu and that Larry, Owen, Mike Reynolds or myself couldn't back him up with. One of us would always be able to come up with enough of it to jump in and help him out.

One time after we'd been playing a game in Montgomery I took those guys over to Selma for a night. Introduced them to a bunch of my hometown friends at one of the bars there, a place called Charlie Brown's. Pretty soon we had everybody interested in this little

"Stump Stu" game of ours. We must have played for a couple of hours, right on down to closing time. Everybody in town —- well, everybody in that bar, anyway — was jumping around and having a great time, trying to stump us. Of course, they couldn't do it. We never did get stumped out there, which made us pretty proud.

That night we just wanted to keep on singing and carrying on. We took off from Charlie Brown's and went out to this other place called Roger's Lounge — nothing more than a little honkytonk hole-in-the-wall out on an Alabama back road, but it stayed open all night. Got out to that little roadhouse and dang if they weren't playing golden oldies out there! That just fired us up all the more, and pretty soon we've got the whole joint laughing and cutting up right along with us. Larry Owen was celebrating his birthday that night. And so now Larry's up on one of the tables in that place, dancing and singing away. A couple of older ladies were in there drinking, these gals were sixty-five, seventy years old if they were a day. And what were they doing? They were singing "Sixteen Candles" to Larry, for all they were worth! I'll have to say it was one of the funniest things I ever saw. We stayed in there cutting up and singing for just hours and hours. When it came time to go, we said our goodbyes, walked over to the front door to leave, threw that door open and got hit by a flood of bright sunshine. People were blinking and yelling out, "Shut the door!" It was already past seven o'clock in the morning. We'd been having too much fun, we had no idea of the time.

When we got back to my house that morning, we grabbed a little bit of sleep and then my mom put on the best lunch those boys had ever eaten. They were going at that food so hard it was making them break out in a sweat, they couldn't get it in quick enough. Between the good people of Selma, and my mom and daddy's great hospitality, my friends from the Savannah team had one wonderful time on that visit to my home town. If they could have had a choice, I think they'd have moved there right then.

One other night I remember, the bunch of us were out singing after a game in Nashville, Tennessee. This time it wasn't any kind of special celebration, we'd been playing ball all night long and were just out for a bite to eat and a beer or two. We found this little place there in Nashville called Frank and Steins. They had beans, hot dogs, cold beer, everything we wanted. We were all on a pretty tight budget but it was pretty cheap in there, so we got to eating and drinking away. We had a curfew, we were supposed to be getting back to the hotel, but I don't think we made it. Because walking back, we came across this multilevel parking garage that was just made for singing. Concrete walls all around, giving you great echoes. We got in there and realized we had an echo chamber working. Pretty soon we were harmonizing away. Seeing us singing and carrying on in there you'd have thought it was something in a movie — you know, street guys on a corner with trash cans burning and everybody singing and harmonizing along. We'd never found better acoustics than we had inside that parking lot in Nashville. When I think back now on how much fun the four of us had singing together, that might be my best memory of all.

Body and Soul

Being ballplayers, wherever we went we were always on the lookout for really good places to eat that weren't too expensive. A great place we found in downtown Savannah was Mrs. Wilkes' Boarding House. They had these all-you-could-eat meals served up family-style. You'd sit down at a table, they'd bring you your serving of meat and then they'd have big bowls of vegetables, five or six different vegetables, rolls and stuff all around. After that they'd bring a couple of different desserts. And you had your iced tea, just like sitting around the dinner table at home. Then when you got through eating, you picked up your plate, took it back to the kitchen, emptied the leavings in a trashcan and put the plate in the sink, where somebody would be there to wash it for you.

It was just like being at home; in fact I think a big part of the reason a lot of the guys liked that place was because it really did remind them of home. Most of the players on that Savannah club were real young, eighteen, nineteen, twenty. They needed that good food. A lot of the younger guys followed along after us to Mrs. Wilkes' Boarding House. You got tired of those 7-11 burritos and hot dogs all the time, that place was a nice change for everybody and we really did enjoy it.

A minor league ballplayer always has to struggle to hold body and soul together. It seemed like about half our time on road trips was put in on searching out a decent meal. In Jackson, Mississippi, we were happy to find a place somewhat along the same lines as Mrs. Wilkes' Boarding House. It was called The White House. A colonial-style place right downtown close to the business district of Jackson — a lot of the local businessmen ate there. You'd be seated at these great big round wooden tables. The center of the table was moveable, like a lazy susan. That center part would spin around. All the food was placed out there in big bowls. If you wanted something, instead of asking to have it passed around, you'd just spin the table. The bowl you wanted would come rolling around, and as it went by you'd grab it and help yourself. Table kept right on going around, and when the empty spot came back you'd replace that bowl and pick out another one. Just delicious food — my, I used to love to go down there. It was a real treat, a piece of true Southern culture.

Character

Each level of baseball turns up the pressure on you in a new way. Double-A bus rides are longer than the ones in Single-A. If you're not man enough to take those marathon bus rides, then the system doesn't want you. They're judging character, here. You've got to be able to handle the strain of the long tough rides and be able to get yourself up to play the next night. A couple of hours of groggy sleep in the hotel, a bite to eat in a greasy spoon somewhere, get back out on the field and perform. Your job depends on going out to do it every single night. Everybody knows that if you don't do well, you won't advance. In the minor leagues there are always a million people trying to get in and take that one job. For a player like me, there was never any question about doing your best every time. The element of struggle was always there. But the things that made that bush league life tough are mixed up really very closely with the good things that you remember. Nobody having any luxuries, nobody having enough money to do anything without the other guys around, everybody sticking together, making up your own fun — it was a little like a soldier's situation during a war, everybody bonding together and getting real tight just so as to survive it.

Good Things in Savannah

Before I get off the subject of living in Savannah, there were two wonderful things I discovered there. One little thing, one big.

The first thing I discovered in that town was the joy of chicken fingers. Though I lived to eat, somehow I hadn't experienced that particular delicacy before. I loved those things so much. We'd all head over to a place called Spanky's late at night after games. We would have just a ball sitting in there. They'd have big pitchers of beer and you'd get buckets of nice crispy tender chicken fingers, which you dipped in this delicious honey-mustard sauce. I could have sat there and eaten those lovely little things forever.

More importantly, I met Chris McCowan in Savannah. Chris had come up to Savannah from Florida with a girlfriend of hers who was visiting one of my roommates. They'd all met up while we were in spring training down at West Palm Beach. Chris was a real quiet girl, a little bit older, and coming off a divorce just then. She was three years older than me, and I was a half-dozen years older than most of the other players there at Savannah. She didn't care much for some of the younger players she'd met, so pretty soon the two of us found ourselves getting fixed up together. We went out and had a good time, me doing my usual singing along with the band and carrying on and her saying a total of about six words.

Chris went back down to Florida. Later on she came out once with her girlfriend to a game we played in Orlando against the Twins' Double-A team in that town. Then I didn't see her again for a real long time. I figured she had got married again, because when I would call the number she had given me, a guy would always answer the phone. I'd hang up, not knowing what to say. Once I did talk to the guy, but I didn't even leave my number. So I was out of touch with her that whole long time.

Two years went by, and then I had left the Braves and had been picked up by the Mets, and was with them down in spring training.

I got to signing autographs for a bunch of kids at the ballpark one day. A big bunch of kids around me, all chattering at me, and I'm there with my head down, just minding my business, signing away. Behind me I hear a different voice, not a kid's this time but a woman's. "Would you mind signing my thigh?" Boy, I'll tell you my head snapped right around in a heartbeat. There was Chris, standing there, looking right at me and looking real beautiful. I got interested all over again.

We started dating, and like a lot of minor league courtships it was on and off for quite a while, but finally we got hitched in 1985. We agreed if we ever had a little girl we'd name her after the place where we'd first met; we thought that it was just such a beautiful city, and we'd had such fine times there. Four years after we were married Chris got pregnant and we were blessed with that little girl. Savannah was born in 1989. She's growing up now and she's just as lovely as her name. Someday we're going to take her back over to Savannah, Georgia, and show her all around the beautiful sights of that town.

Part Five
Moving Up

Give Me a Chance Before You Say I Can't

I was in Savannah from '78 to '80, as I've said. Each year now my arm was getting back a little more strength. My innings went up every year — from 67 at Greenwood in '77, to 91 at Savannah and Kinston in '78, 106 at Savannah and Richmond in '79, 145 at Savannah and Jackson in '80. I pitched fairly well and always had pretty good stats, but it seemed like a lot of people thought Double-A was going to be my high water level. I'd get bounced up and down in the Atlanta system, from Double-A down to Single-A in '78, from Double-A up to Triple-A in '79, then back down to Double-A again in '80. And at that point the Braves released me. I guess they figured I was never going to be good enough to stay up any higher. But looking back, it's pretty easy to see that in the Atlanta organization the cards were stacked against me that whole time.

There's an invisible class system that runs through minor league baseball, you see. In every big league system you're going to run into an unspoken prejudice against the undrafted player. Your undrafted people are not going to get the same treatment as your prospects, the guys that represent your biggest stake in scouting time and money. Your "projects" are just not going to get an equal shot. They've got to do better, just to become equal.

So I kind of floated along for a few years there with Atlanta — always seeing other players get moved up, while I just drifted around that Double-A level. After a while I didn't really expect to get promoted any more, to tell you the truth. I could see that with Atlanta, as an undrafted player I was always going to be stuck at the bottom of the barrel. It was not just me. On the Savannah team we had a couple of other guys who hadn't been drafted; whenever the call-ups came, we were always the ones who were going to get passed over. Whoever the organization had their money invested in was going to get to go up first.

Later on, after I'd finally made it to the big leagues with the Mets, I got a call over the winter back home in Selma from one of the Atlanta scouts who'd first signed me. I should have been in the majors two or three years earlier, that man told me. He said he didn't know why the Braves had never brought me up. Well, the fact is, there was a line of order. I was way down in the line, and as long as I was down there, I had no choice but to hang on and deal with it. We had a saying at Double-A, that we had to do twice as good twice as long, just to get noticed, just to get moved up.

And like I say, it wasn't just the Atlanta organization that did things that way. In '82, when I was at the Triple-A level with the Mets and was pitching very well, the big league team needed a pitcher. Now my coaches down there seemed pretty happy with how I was doing, partly because it showed how even an undrafted guy might be able to get ahead. And furthermore I wasn't the only pitcher down there who'd been working pretty hard for quite a while. But when the call-up came, the guy the Mets brought up was a prospect from down in Double-A. They just jumped over everybody from the Triple-A level. They brought in Doug Sisk. Dougie was a pretty good pitcher, he had great stuff and he stayed up in the big leagues for a while. But at the time it happened I didn't even know him. All I knew about it was that I'd just got passed over again.

So here I'd started out just wanting to see if I could make it to Double-A, because in the beginning I'd never really been sure how good I was. Sometimes I remembered an incident that had occurred at one point while I was still in college. I ran into a couple of guys I had played against when they were at the University of Alabama. They had gone on to play a little minor league ball. They saw me pitch, and they told me they thought I didn't have the greatest talent, but it looked like I had a lot of guts. Thinking about that comment helped keep me going. Once I'd got to Double-A and shown that I was good enough to stay there, I wasn't going to set limits on myself. I'd say, "If I'm doing good here, you can't tell me I can't go ahead and move up a little higher. The only way you can tell me that is if I go up there and prove that I can't do it. Give me a chance before you say I can't."

Odd Man Out

The funny part of it is, I was actually pitching very well with Savannah in 1980, when Atlanta released me. The things I had going against me were that I hadn't been drafted, I was twenty-seven years old, and I had a history of arm trouble. That season I'd been doing a little starting and a little relieving. I would start a game, a couple of days later I'd get used in relief, a couple of days after that I would start again. I gave them the innings, did everything they asked. My stats were just fine. I had a 5-1 record when they called me in and told me the ax was coming down.

The way it went was this. They had four number one draft picks they had to place in the organization that season. They already had a number one pick, Tim Cole. And now they had three more guys they'd drafted in the first round, Craig McMurtry, Jim Acker and Ken Dayley. All three of those guys were going to be placed at Double-A. And down there we had Steve Bedrosian, Bedrock was already eating up a whole lot of innings. We had Duane Theiss, who later made it up to the big leagues for a while. Jim Bouton came through, pitched with us on his comeback. Bouton got to go up. Stu Livingstone got to move up to Triple-A, but that was fine with me because Stu was one of us. He'd worked real hard, and when he got to go up, that was cool. We were all working hard, for that matter. Lord, I can't even remember who all was there, but when we had to fit in those three first round picks, somebody's number had to come up. The odd man out turned out to be me.

Did they figure I was damaged goods? I don't know. I'd been giving them all those innings, starting and relief, whatever they asked me. About mid-season my arm started hurting a little bit again, just because I'd been pitching so much. At that point I was rapidly catching up to Bedrosian in most innings. Yet I was still throwing the ball very well. Bob Veale, who was the Braves' travelling pitching coach, came through Savannah about that time and talked to me. I mentioned to him that my arm was hurting, and he talked about how to go about resting it. I said, "Well, I'm pitching tonight." He just walked off shaking his head. "You tell me you're hurting, and you're pitching tonight? What the hell are you talking about?" Then two days later he drifted through again. I was warming up to go into another game. "Didn't you tell me your arm was hurting?" "Well, yeah," I said, "but I've got to…" And he just cut me off. "No one's going to look after that arm but you," he said. Well, I couldn't afford to rest it. My job was on the line, I just kept going. And my arm did get better, to where it wasn't hurting me any more. It was just at that point, with a little over a month to go in the season, that they gave me my release notice.

At the time it happened we were on the road. We had just bussed our tails all the way over to Knoxville. Fell out of the bus, got out to the ballpark, the game was just about to start. Eddie Haas, the manager, called me in and dropped the bomb. I'll have to admit it came as a real shock to me. My friends on that Savannah team were pretty upset too, they hated to see me go. But what could I do? I tried to talk to Eddie. I said, "Eddie, is there any point in my trying to come back? Should I keep trying? Is this it? Am I done?" Because that's my Double-A dream that just went down the tube, my dream of being a big league ballplayer. And Eddie said, "No, I don't think you can make it. Your fastball's not good enough. Your slider's too flat. I just don't think that stuff will ever cut it in the major leagues. I don't think you've got a shot."

A year after that day I was up in the big leagues with the Mets. You can't always listen to what people tell you, you have to do what you feel.

A Fresh Start

The Mets picked me up for that last month or so, and I ended up going 5-1 for their Double-A team over in Jackson. That meant I was 10-2 in Double-A that season. It was a pretty good year for a guy who didn't have a shot.

How did I get over to Jackson? Well, I think Eddie Haas wanted to help me out, after all. Eddie put in a couple of calls, trying to find me something. And it turned out right at that time the Mets had just shipped a pitcher up from Jackson to Triple-A. It was Rick Anderson, who later became a good friend of mine. Of course, I didn't know him back then. All I knew was that a guy had gone up and that left a vacancy at Jackson, and they were going to take me to fill his spot.

Bill Monbouquette, who was the pitching coach over there with the Mets, had wanted them to trade for me before, I later found out. I got this part of the story from talking with Bill a couple of years ago. It's the kind of story that makes you stop and wonder how personnel decisions in baseball are really made. You see, the Mets had actually already made some kind of an offer to trade for me, and the Braves had turned them down. So now the Mets signed me, and I'd been pitching for them at Jackson about a week, when Bill Monbouquette got a call about me from Hank Aaron of the Braves. It seems Hank was unaware that his own club had already released me and that I was already over there pitching at Jackson. He asked Bill Monbouquette if the Mets were still interested in making a deal for me. I guess the Braves weren't exactly keeping up with things in their own organization. "I informed Hank you were already on our team," Bill told me.

Help Yourself!

Getting myself over to Jackson took several stops. The Braves had given me a plane ticket from Knoxville back to Savannah. When I got to Savannah, Eddie Haas called me and told me to get in touch with these people with the Mets. I packed up my stuff from out of that duplex by the beach, jumped in my car, drove from Savannah to Selma, spent the night with my parents, then the next day drove on into Jackson. Met the general manager there, and then they put me on a plane that flew me out to Midland, Texas, where the team was playing. In that little bitty Midland clubhouse I had my introductions to my new teammates. The place was almost too small to turn around in, and all the lockers were taken. There was absolutely no room. I looked around and nobody said a word. But then Jesse Orosco came up to me and said, "Come on, you can share my locker with me." I had no idea who the guy was at the time, but from then on he and I were real close. We became roommates along the way, and always got along well — Jesse is just a super-nice person. Well, as time went on the guys were all pretty nice to me over there, but when I was stuck that first day in the locker room without a place to put my clothes, there was nobody else who said anything. Only Jesse. He just jumped right out, you know, "Help yourself!" He was the first guy who made me feel at home.

The Hitters Aren't Seeing It

When I got over there to Jackson they made a starter out of me. I might have pitched once in relief to get my feet wet, or maybe made one start that was a no-decision. Then I settled in and clicked off five winning starts in a row, finished three of those, even tossed in a couple of shutouts. I can't remember when I'd last pitched a shutout before that — certainly not since college.

The second shutout I threw, the head of the Mets' minor league system happened to be watching. As soon as I came off the field, he pulled me over. He told me I'd thrown pretty well but I was telegraphing my pitches. "You know, from up in the stands I could call every pitch you were throwing to those hitters." "Well, maybe you could," I told him. "But they couldn't." My second consecutive complete game shutout, I guess I felt like I had things working pretty good. "I don't mind somebody seeing things from the stands as long as the hitters can't see from where they are," I told him. I can't even remember that minor league director's name right now, it's been too long, I only see his face.

That was my next-to-last game of the year. 1980 had turned out pretty well for me after all. Here I was throwing exactly the same way at Jackson that I'd been throwing at Savannah. Same stuff, same level, same competition both places. One place, they told me my career was over. The other place, I thought maybe I was on my way.

Stranger in a Strange Land (Colombia, 1980)

After that season I went down to Colombia and got my first taste of winter ball — and of life outside the United States. I was definitely a stranger in a strange land.

The Mets asked me to go down there. It didn't take me very long to make up my mind. That fall I had picked up a little job at my dad's cotton company. I was a squidge, as they called it, the lowest guy on the totem pole, a guy who does a whole lot of work and earns very little money. I was making $4 an hour as a squidge at the time I got asked to go to Colombia. Down there I'd be getting a free apartment, meal money and one thousand tax-free dollars per month. It took me about one second to decide to accept that offer.

The Colombian league season was getting going, they wanted me down there right away. I had to get up real early, catch a bus from Selma into Birmingham, fly to Atlanta, lay over there a couple of hours, then fly down to Miami. I had another layover in Miami, where I had to get my paperwork done to leave the country. I went downtown and located the Federal Building but then I couldn't find my way to the Colombian consulate. Now already here in Miami I was running into nothing but Spanish-speaking people, and I didn't speak a word of Spanish. I said, This is going to be a long trip.

Went out to the airport. Plane's delayed, they tell me. I was at the Miami airport for fourteen hours, just sitting around waiting. They said something was wrong with the plane. From the waiting area you could look right into the cockpit. I took a look, all I could see was feet. They had a bunch of guys down on the floor of the cockpit, working. I said, I don't know if I want to be getting on this plane.

Finally we did get off the ground. Three and a half hours later I'm in Colombia. Now I'd been awake almost two days. A guy picked me up at the airport in this beat-up old car. It was sultry, muggy hot — maybe two, three o'clock in the morning. Driving through these dark back streets. Finally I get dropped off at this apartment complex. My apartment is on the eighth floor, the electricity is out. Now it's four o'clock in the morning. I've got to carry all my luggage up eight floors. Man, I was dying. The pair of boots I was wearing hadn't been off my feet for about twenty-five hours. Dragging my weary tail into that apartment, I didn't know any of the guys, but at that point I didn't care — I just crashed.

After getting a merciful day off to rest up a little, I went out and met my team. Some pretty good players, basically equivalent to a Double-A level club. We had Dale Mohorcik, Jesse Barfield, Rick Lancellotti. I was sharing a two-bedroom apartment with three guys from the Pirates organization. We stuck together pretty much when we weren't on the baseball field. We'd get through playing ball, come home and entertain ourselves the best we could. We'd play Monopoly. We'd play three complete games of Monopoly in one night. Man, that time could go slow down in Colombia. When we got tired of playing Monopoly we'd go to this little place down the road, just this little hole in the wall where you could rustle up some beer. Then we'd go back and play some more Monopoly. We'd play until four, five in the morning. We'd watch the sun come up, playing Monopoly.

We were in Baranquilla, a big dirty town. That league had five teams in two towns, Baranquilla and Cartagena. You bounced back and forth on a bus between those two places, making stops in every little village along the way. That was a real experience — you've got to back up about a hundred years to get a picture of what it was like. You'd make a stop in some little dirty town at a crossroads in the middle of nowhere. Mud streets, pigs running in and out of houses squealing, smoke and grease filling the air from people frying up foods. The houses were built out of three-or-four-inch-diameter logs, stacked up with mud packed in between to hold them together. Mud roof. Inside, there'd be one light bulb. A black-and-white TV, and a whole houseful of kids sitting around on a mud floor watching it.

The owner of our team had a place out on this little inlet, Santa Marta — it's the local resort area, with a beach and night clubs. The man would give the American players the team bus, throw in a case of beer and send us down to stay at his beach condo for three or four days. We'd relax at the beach, take a little break. It was our R & R. I'll never forget our manager, Tommy Zandt, coming down there with us and imposing his version of team discipline on us. Tommy was a real nut. He'd actually fine you five dollars if he caught you on the beach at Santa Marta without a beer in your hands.

I stayed down there in Colombia for three or four months, right on past Christmas and New Year's. I ended up pitching a whole lot, about 110 innings, and I pitched real well. But that was one place I played where baseball was not really the hardest part of the job. It was adjusting to a whole other way of life that was the biggest challenge. I went on in later years to play winter ball in Venezuela, Puerto Rico and the Dominican Republic, but in terms of all the places I went, Colombia was definitely the hardest. Like I say, you're going to have to back up about a hundred years if you're going to adjust to living down there. It's their culture, you have to do like they do. It's definitely a challenge, and a real learning event. Some people learned real quick and just got right in sync with it. I remember Rick Lancellotti loved to go down and haggle with all the dealers in the black market. Rick was a city kid from back East. I was just a country boy from Alabama, for me fitting-in took a little bit more work.

You Can Pitch

The next season, 1981, I went to my first spring training with the Mets. That was the beginning of a real long year of pitching for me. I pitched in Double-A, Triple-A, and the major leagues that season, a total of 169 innings, the most in my career. Then when the season was over I went down to winter ball in Caracas, Venezuela, and pitched some more.

I started with the Norfolk / Tidewater Triple-A squad in the spring. Jack Aker, the Mets' Triple-A manager, had been a little bit of a sidearmer himself, and I think he had visions of me coming on as a sidearm closer, a big save guy. But for some reason I don't think I impressed him right off the bat up there. I stayed around for a month or so, didn't get a whole lot of throwing in, pitched so-so, and then got sent back down to Double-A.

Davey Johnson was the manager at Jackson, when I got back down there. Davey made me a starter again. His encouragement was very important to me, and I pitched very well for him. I won five games down there for him, before going back up to Tidewater.

One time down in Double-A that May, Davey Johnson and I were sitting around in this tiny little bar in some town on the road when Davey said to me, "You can pitch." I'll never forget that. This place was just a ten-foot-square room with a bar and maybe five chairs. We were talking on about this and that, about the different levels of baseball and what you needed to succeed at each one. In the course of that conversation Davey told me he saw no reason why I couldn't go back up to Triple-A and do well there and then go on to pitch in the major leagues. "I know you can do it," he told me, "and I think you should, because you can pitch. You can be a major league pitcher." It was the first time anybody who really knew what they were talking about had ever said that to me. You can believe it made me feel good.

We were playing a game in June out in Tulsa, against the Rangers' farm team there. I started it, had put in nine innings and had a shutout going. A zero-zero tie, and I'm on my way out to pitch the tenth when Davey stops me. "You're not going back out." I couldn't believe it. "But I feel fine!" I wanted to finish up that shutout. Davey said, "No, you can't go back out there." I said, "Davey, I don't care what you say, I'm going back out." He said, "No, you can't, because all you're supposed to be doing tonight is getting your work in. They want you to be able to pitch again in a few days up in Tidewater." So I let him win that argument!

Scared and Happy

That rise up from Double-A to Triple-A to the majors over a couple of months in 1981 happened so fast, it was a whirl. When I got back to Tidewater in June, this time I didn't feel so out of place pitching in Triple-A. Each new league I'd moved up to, I'd had trouble adjusting. Thinking that everybody else was better than me was always my biggest problem. It was a simple confidence thing. I didn't go into new situations with the right frame of mind. Instead of just saying, "Let's go get it done," I was being too defensive, and that was definitely holding me back. So when I went back up to Tidewater, and then went on up to the Mets that same year, I kind of resolved to attack everything a little bit harder. I had in mind what Davey Johnson had said to me, and also a little advice I got from my brother Alan, who said, "Don't be impressed, be impressive." That's the kind of thinking I was going to need to be doing now.

I was 5-2 back in Triple-A. Jack Aker had me relieving there, then he had me back starting. When I went up to the Mets, I was back to relieving again. I didn't care what they threw at me, now.

The major league strike that was going on that year ended, and when they started playing again in August, a couple of people on the Mets got hurt, and I got the call. It was a complete surprise to me, I hadn't expected it at all. I was finally going where I'd always wanted to be, though I'd never really dared to let myself believe I'd actually get there. At the time I got the word we were in Charleston, West Virginia, on the last day of a long, hard road trip. I had no money, no clean clothes. In those days I had myself duded-up with a perm. By the end of this trip the perm was totally blown out. I had an old straw cowboy hat I wore to try to cover up that disaster on the top of my head. I had my jeans, I was a real lonesome cowboy. I mean I was looking seriously bad.

I was also seriously happy. I was scared and happy at the same time, but I was more happy. The phone rang in my hotel room at seven o'clock in the morning, Jack Aker telling me I had a flight to Chicago to meet up with the New York club. Be there on time for that day's game. I threw together my stuff so fast! Leaped into a taxi, rushed to the airport, flew to Chicago, landed, found a cab. On the way from O'Hare airport out to Wrigley Field that cab had a flat tire. Things happen for a reason. But why now, Lord? I jump out, help the guy whip off the old tire, slam the spare tire on. Finally I get to the park. It's a half hour before game time, they won't let me in the gate. Here I am, in my amazing minor league attire. I'm not down on any list, the ushers don't have any idea who I am. I've got tire dirt on my hands now, my gear is falling out all over the place. "But I've got all my baseball stuff here, see? I'm a player. You've got to let me in!"

At last they figure it out. Someone from the team comes down. We go in the locker room. They put me right next to Dave Kingman. "Hi, Kong, howya doing?" Kong is sitting there not saying much, intimidating and a little removed. This was a veteran who'd earned his space. I had the feeling I should really just leave the area and give the man some room.

Joe Torre was the manager. I was ready to play. At that point I didn't know how many days I was going to be in the major leagues, or how many games I was going to get to play in. It turned out I was up there for 58 days that year, which was how long the season lasted, and got into 21 games. But that first day, Joe Torre held me out, probably out of kindness. He just wanted to let me kind of get my bearings. Then the next day he threw me right into a game in relief.

Ed Lynch still gets on me about that game, my big league debut. Ed had a win coming in that game, it may have been his first win. At that point Joe Torre brought me in. I think it was the eighth inning, we were leading by a run. Two outs, man on second. Mike Lum hit a pinch hit two-run homer off me. We lost the lead, Ed lost the win, I lost the save. We came back to win the game though, so I didn't have to feel completely bad. I think Ed Lynch may have held it against me forever, though, deep in his mind. He jokes about it, but I wonder. One time a while back I called him about a job with the Cubs, it didn't work out.

Oh, I was more scared than happy when I got out on the mound that day. Going into a major league park made a big, big difference. Close game, and the people were really loud, because of the big rivalry the Cubs have with the Mets. I was shaking when Mike Lum hit that home run.

I guess I felt like a fish out of water in the big leagues for my first few weeks. Well, I might have been old for a rookie, but I was still a rookie, after all. As I say, I didn't have any clothes with me, and we were out on the road. I had to borrow stuff from other guys. I put together a hand-me-down outfit, black pants, dark navy blue shirt, black tie, black coat. People might have mistaken me for a country undertaker, because all I was able to scrounge up were these dark clothes. All through that trip, I was one surprisingly ugly rookie. Hadn't yet got my first paycheck, but I had to do something. What I did finally was take my meal money — a couple of days' big league meal money actually came to more than my whole Triple-A paycheck — and go out and buy myself a whole new wardrobe with that. I might have been hungry by the time we got back to New York, but you can bet I looked a whole lot better than when I came in.

Accustoming myself to the big leagues was going to take a little bit of doing. At first everything scares you a little. I got a little bit more comfortable, though, with each time I got to pitch. My next time out, I actually got to start. Another dream. It was against Philadelphia. I went five innings, gave up only one unearned run.

The game was at Shea. Standing out there on the mound, getting ready to make my first pitch, all I could say to myself was, "Man, I'm in *way* over my head, I've got no idea what's going on! I'm supposed to be in the major leagues now, starting a game — whoa, it's pretty scary!" It's New York, you know, it's a full house. I glance up at the stands, all these people are looking down at me. The next thing I notice is the Phils' leadoff hitter stepping in, and

of course it would be Pete Rose. Welcome to the big show, kid —
Pete's looking out at me with this hard little stare, half checking me
out, half laughing at me. And Pete's got it right: I'm just this little
fat kid from Alabama, who's got no idea what he's doing there.

At that moment my heart was going about a thousand miles an
hour, my knees were wobbling around like a jello mold in an earth-
quake, I was sweating cold bullets and having a real hard time getting my breath. I was trying to *look* calm, but it was a struggle. Then
I threw Pete a pitch or two, and he kind of did a little double take.
Obviously I looked a little bit different to him — he definitely was-
n't used to seeing my kind of sidearm stuff. On one pitch my ball
would rise up on him a little bit, then the next one it would sink.
You don't see that too much, even in the major leagues. After a few
pitches Pete hit a ground ball down to second base and got thrown
out, no problem. Right at that point I thought, "Hey, maybe I *do*
belong in the big leagues." I picked up my first little bit of confidence right there. And you know, a couple of years later Pete Rose
came out in an interview in *Sports Illustrated* with his list of the
toughest pitchers that he had to face. Come to find out, Terry Leach
landed up there in the top five. I think Pete had about half a dozen
at bats against me in my first two seasons in the National League,
and he struck out at least three times. Pete never struck out very
much, so that's pretty fair pitching.

One other thing in particular stands out in my memory of that
first start. The main guy in the Philadelphia lineup at that time was
Mike Schmidt. The man was a real major league stud hitter. I think
he led the league in home runs and runs batted in, that year. Right
now he's in the Hall of Fame. Well, that night when I was down in
the bullpen warming up, just trying to stay as calm as I could and
work with the best stuff that I had, the one hitter I was going to
have to face who was really on my mind was Mike Schmidt. So at
one point I looked over between pitches at the bullpen coach who
was standing beside me, and I said, "Okay, imagine this is Mike

Schmidt hitting right now: I've got a one-ball, two-strike count, and here's what I'm going to do to him." And I brought in a nasty slider that would have been right on the black, right-hand corner, if my catcher had been behind home plate. Boy, that was a nice pitch. And the coach said, "It would be mighty fine if you could do that during the game."

Well, as fate would have it, there I am pitching the game, Mike Schmidt comes up to hit against me, I go to a one-ball, two-strike count on him. Said to myself, "Well, let's see if I *can* do that." Threw my next pitch, a real nice little slider. Ooh, nasty pitch, right on the black, breaking hard. Swing and a miss. Mike Schmidt turns around and walks back to the dugout with the bat on his shoulder, which for a hitter is a kind of unintentional way of showing a certain respect. I *did* punch out Mike Schmidt, just like I said I was going to. Made me very proud.

After that one start I went back and worked out of the bullpen. When you're a reliever, it's kind of like you're still a virgin until you get thrown into your first real pressure situation, some spot where a game is actually on the line. The first crucial situation Joe Torre got me into was in a game against the Cincinnati Reds, the team that had the best record in the league in that abbreviated season. The Reds had loaded the bases with two out, late in a tied-up game. The guy Joe Torre brought me in to face in that spot was George Foster, who was probably one-two with Mike Schmidt as the most dangerous hitter in the National League at that time. This was just a couple of years after Foster had had that ungodly season, fifty-two dingers, 149 r.b.i.'s. He was a serious load — something to be feared a little bit, right there. Tight game, bases loaded, two out, big George coming up: for a rookie to be put into this situation was definitely a baptism by fire.

I couldn't help being scared, but then again I was also really excited to be getting this chance. I started out being a little bit cautious, pretty soon I'd run the count up full. Now I've got this big black bat waggling in my face, George Foster glaring out at me, three balls and two strikes, the runners getting nervous feet and dancing off the bases. I threw a fastball that he was just a *hair* away from timing. He uncoiled on it, but just missed it and fouled it off. Don't try that again. Now came the moment of truth. A rookie pitcher throwing a three-two breaking ball to the most feared hitter in the league with the bases loaded, that's not something you're going to see every day. And I think this was another one of the moments that helped make me into a pitcher up there, gave me the confidence to believe I *could* pitch in the major leagues. I threw him a slider. Big George stood there frozen stiff like a piece of ice sculpture as that pitch broke right over the corner for a called third strike. Right there I learned a very important lesson. I said to myself, "Boy, what this means is you've got to have guts up here. When they give you your chance and throw you out there, you can't choke up, you've got to let that talent flow."

Excited, scared, happy, a little bit proud — I ran through all those feelings more than once, before that season was over. By the end of it I was feeling less scared than happy, no contest. Had a few things to be happy about, after all. I definitely hadn't embarrassed myself. Did everything they'd asked me to. Pitched thirty-five innings, gave up only twenty-six hits, had a 2.57 e.r.a., which was just one point off the lowest earned run average on the Mets' staff. Didn't give up a run in any of my home appearances at Shea Stadium, which the newspapers picked up and made a nice little thing out of. I was happy most of all to have stuck with the way I was doing things, got to the big leagues, and just stayed up.

Big League Money

The minimum wage in the big leagues at that time was $40,000. It's not really that much money — even back then it wasn't that much. But to me, after all those years beating around the bushes, it looked like a fortune. The taxes they were taking out of a single big league check came to more than I had ever made in one paycheck in the minors. Two months of that big league money and I thought I was as rich as one of the Rockefellers.

Went down to Venezuela after the season and pitched a little bit for a team in Caracas. Pretty good league they had down there, quite a few major league players. I shared a condo on the thirty-second floor of a Caracas high-rise with some other American guys from my team, Dave Henderson, Ron Gardenhire, Joe Cowley. A few of the guys playing down there were local heroes, Venezuelan players who'd made good in the U. S. I'll never forget the way the fans treated those guys — Bo Diaz, Tony Armas, they were regular superstars down there. Tony Armas would be standing out in the outfield during a game and all of a sudden here would come some kid running out of the stands to get his autograph. Right in the middle of the game — I couldn't get over that. Tony would sign. The game would keep going on. Pretty soon, here comes another kid dashing out to him for an autograph. Down there Tony was a real culture hero. In fact he'd actually led the American League in home runs during that shortened season, and also led the league in strikeouts. He did the same thing down there, I guess. People certainly loved him whatever he did. Maybe for an established guy like Tony the glory he got down there was as good as the money. Me, I wasn't getting any glory. I didn't get to pitch much, didn't do too well, and got sent home before the playoffs. But I did get to expand my cultural horizons another little bit, and even more important, I got to add something to my little baseball nest-egg.

When I got back home, I figured I'd stick to my usual little economy. Said to myself, "Well, I'll be at home, I'll live for free, I'll eat for free, I'll get a little job, I'll put away my money. Fifteen hundred dollars should get me through the winter." Well, somehow or other when you've made it to the big leagues everybody in the world seems to know it. Now you have to treat everybody big league style. You end up buying a lot of rounds of beer for people. That winter I was buying a whole lot of rounds for a whole lot of people. I think my beer tab at one little bar in town ran up to about $4000 that off-season. I know I didn't drink that much beer myself, but man, *somebody* was enjoying me. I was having a good time treating my friends nice. I figured if I never made it back to the big leagues, I could die happy.

Part Six
The Numbers Game

What Went On?

That next spring of '82 I pitched well in Florida, and for a while things were looking good. When the *New York Times* Sunday magazine came down to take a picture of the new young pitching staff of the Mets, there I was, along with Rick Ownbey, Tim Leary, Ron Darling, Jeff Bittiger, Doug Sisk, Scott Holman. We were supposed to be the young hope coming up right then, the future stars.

I never had much of a chance to shine that spring, as it turned out. Got cut before the team went north. What went on? They said it was because they couldn't make a trade. They had an infielder they wanted to trade, but they couldn't close the deal and wound up having to keep him. Now they were short a roster spot, and the season was about to start. They had to keep an extra infielder, so they had to cut the pitching staff from ten down to nine. Somebody had to go back to Triple-A. I got my walking papers.

When they told me I was gone, it was eleven o'clock on a Saturday night. I was booked on a Sunday morning flight to New York. Already had my tickets and everything. I'd left my car with a company that was going to drive it up north. All my stuff was already shipped on ahead, except what I had in one suitcase. When I got the news, I had to go steal my car out of the parking lot at that driveaway place. I needed it to get me to Tidewater. The whole deal was pretty upsetting.

Sink or Swim

I pitched half a season at Tidewater. Forty-nine innings, 2.96 e.r.a. with five saves. Davey Johnson, who'd now moved up to manage there, had always liked to pitch me a lot. When he was managing me later on with the Mets he would say I liked to be abused, because I could throw and throw and throw, and then come back and throw some more. Davey really liked that in me. So I was pitching a lot for him, my arm was holding up, and I was doing well enough down at Tidewater to get back up to New York before long.

I got into twenty-one big league games that summer, but didn't really distinguish myself much until the last series of the season. October 1, 1982. We were in Philadelphia. Rick Ownbey was scheduled to start that night.

Now Rick was a very funny guy, he used to crack me up — a seriously warped person. He was a blond-haired California beach kid who was always cutting up. We'd played together in Triple-A, and down there he was practically a legend — I remember one time we were playing the Yanks' farm team over at Columbus, our big brass from New York had come in for the game, everybody's on best behavior, and here's Rick out in the bullpen putting on this crazy comedy show during a rain delay, twirling these white towels around in the air in a perfect imitation of a guy bringing a helicopter in for a landing. Rick was actually a bonafide frisbee master; he could throw a frisbee with his toes. He was also a world-class hackysack kicker. He had all these useless talents. As a pitcher he always had great stuff, but he had terrible control problems. After we all went out to see that movie *Rocky* Rick had a great line: "I'm the eye of the tiger with the control of a newt." One of the funniest people I've ever met, Rick Ownbey. But when Rick came up with a blister and couldn't pitch that day, it was no joke. They threw me into his starting spot.

It had been a long time since I had started anything. There was no way I was thinking of myself as a starting pitcher. I had not pitched more than four innings in any game that year. Then again, I wasn't afraid of starting, either. I saw this as a lucky chance, and I was determined to make the most of it.

There was no particular pressure on me to win the game — we weren't in contention for anything, in fact we were dead last, about eight games behind the next team ahead of us. But for me there was some personal incentive to pitch well, because I *did* have something to contend for. It wasn't too hard to see that by throwing me out there they were just giving me enough rope to hang myself. There was a question in everybody's mind whether I was good enough to stay with the organization. Either I'd do well in that start and get to stay, or I'd do badly and give them an excuse to ease me on out by proving that I didn't really belong there. I could just hear them — "If he doesn't do well, he's gone." It was definitely sink or swim.

Well, I knew all that, but then right at the moment there really wasn't enough time for me to worry about it. I had to go on out and warm up. And fortunately, I felt very loose and relaxed from the first pitch I threw in the bullpen. Why I felt so good, I'll never know. When things feel that good, you don't ask questions. Ronn Reynolds, who was catching me down there in the bullpen as I warmed up, told me after the game that he'd had an idea I was going to do something outstanding. "I didn't want to tell you," he said, "but you had some of the best stuff I've ever seen you have."

I took that good bullpen stuff right on into the game with me. For the first few innings, in fact, while I was still strong, it was almost too good. The ball was moving and sinking a *lot*, and because of that I was walking a few people. In the third I walked one guy, the number eight man in the Phils' order, and that upset me enough that I lost concentration for a minute. Tried to pick him off first and threw the ball away, and then I walked the pitcher. Now I was in a little spot, guys on first and third with one out. But I worked out of it, got the next hitter — Gary Maddox I think it was — on a pop fly, and then Pete Rose on a weak little dribbler to the second baseman.

From that point on things just got better and better. I figured out I was wild because I wasn't following through enough to finish up my pitches right. Made a little adjustment on that, and my control improved a lot. I settled in and stuck with the two pitches that were working well for me, my sidearm sinker and my slider. Ron Hodges, who caught me that night, called that slider of mine a "rising up-shoot." Well, I really had it up-shooting that night.

I walked six guys, but I struck out seven. I had such a good feel for the ball that sometimes I'd get a little too nitpicky about hitting a corner, and walk somebody. With the kind of stuff I had that day there was the temptation to nip and tuck, and sometimes I'd get too cocky and miss. But then I'd just come right back and strike somebody out. The top four guys in the Philadelphia order, Maddox, Rose, Gary Matthews and Mike Schmidt, went 0-for-17 against me. That's a fact somebody pointed out to me afterwards. At the time I was in too much of a zone to be worrying a whole lot about who was up.

The one hitter I did have trouble with that night, and this I'll never forget, was Luis Aguayo. This guy was a backup second base-man who'd had maybe fifty at-bats all season. He came up with one out in the fifth and bounced a triple in between the outfielders. That artificial turf will kill you. I got the next two guys out, stranded Aguayo there at third base, and did not give up another hit the rest of the way.

There's one particular pitch I'll always remember from that game, because it was a pitch I'd never thrown before and have never thrown since. It was a slider I threw to Ozzie Virgil, who was the Phils' catcher that night. Now Ozzie had a little bit of a closed stance, where he'd have his left foot planted in closer to the plate than his right. Well, I threw him this amazing slider, which was about half an accident I guess. That pitch kind of slipped out of my hand, and it actually started out behind him. Ozzie saw that and panicked a little. He didn't know where to go, so I guess he just basically folded up. But then all of a sudden the ball broke so sharply that Ron Hodges actually ended up catching it after it came *between* Ozzie's legs. That ball was heading in behind his legs, then literally broke from behind him, went right through his legs, like it was going through a wicket, and ended up in the catcher's glove. I think that pitch scared Ozzie Virgil about halfway to death. And you know it had *me* worried a little bit too, for just a moment. That was one fine breaking slider, right there — sticks out in my mind to this day as one pitch I will always remember, over a whole lot of uglier pitches I've thrown in my life.

Through nine innings I had Philadelphia shut out, but we hadn't scored either. John Denny was pitching for the Phils, and he'd given up only one hit, too. Then in the top of the tenth, Denny came out of the game and we scratched up a run off the guy who replaced him. I was still out there pitching in the bottom of the tenth. To be truthful, I was about ready to collapse. I could hardly breathe. I was bent over resting on my knees between pitches. I was flat worn out, but I sure didn't want to surrender the baseball. I was getting everyone out. I just wanted to finish. I wanted that shutout. I could taste it now, it was that close.

I walked a guy to start the tenth. Aguayo, getting in my hair again. When I went 3-1 on the next batter, I could see our manager, George Bamberger, put one foot up on the dugout step. Another walk and I'd be gone. I came back and got a ground-out, then a soft liner to second base. I got that last out on my last drop of adrenalin. Who hit that little liner — Gary Maddox again? All I remember is seeing Brian Giles at second base close his glove around that third out.

Now, no Mets pitcher has ever pitched a no-hitter, before or since. The last time anybody had pitched even a one-hitter for them was Tom Seaver, five years before. But since I'd gone that extra inning, my ten-inning 1-0 one-hit shutout in that game counted as a team record for low-hit pitching. That record still stands today. It'll be on the books until some Met pitcher of the twenty-first century finally throws a no-no.

Just before the game, when they'd told me I was going to be starting, I'd phoned up my mom and dad — and then I talked to them afterwards, and we shared the high I got from that game. A lot of people in the New York organization hadn't believed I was capable of pitching that well, I know. But down home in Alabama I had people who'd never stopped backing me, and they were really pleased by this. I had friends who'd been my teammates and coaches down there tell me later that they'd been out driving the morning after the game, stopped at McDonald's, got a cup of coffee, bought a paper and hit on that box score. "This has got to be a misprint!" they were saying. A lot of zeroes and just one hit, no runs, ten innings — must be some kind of mistake here! Well, it wasn't a misprint. My ten-inning one-hit game was an actual fact. Those people were real happy for me. They just loved what I'd done. They could appreciate what I'd been through, and where I'd got. I'd sailed through that sink-or-swim game and still had my head above water.

The Numbers Game

Even with that great last game of '82, I ended up down in Norfolk with the Tidewater Triple-A club in the spring of '83. The Mets had brought me back that spring on the strength of my one-hitter, but now they turned around and cut me again. It was the same old thing, the numbers game. Other people were costing them more money and had to be kept. I was no-money-invested, minimum wage, it wasn't going to cost them very much to just hold on to me down at Triple-A as insurance. I was starting to get familiar with that baseball business logic.

Doc

As things turned out, that season they never did need any insurance at the big league level, so I stayed down all year in Tidewater. It was a disappointment not to be going back up, but there were one or two things that happened down there that made the season kind of memorable.

One big thing was getting to watch Dwight Gooden coming on. Doc was just awesome that year after they brought him up from Single-A. He'd come up for the Triple-A playoffs from Lynchburg, where he had pitched about 150 innings and had three-hundred-and-some strikeouts. Lenny Dykstra was playing centerfield behind Doc that year. Doc was just striking out *everybody*, and Lenny, who's a pretty hyper guy, was standing around going nuts, wanting some action. He was all over the Doc about it. He'd scream in at Doc, "Let 'em hit the ball, man! We wanna make it to the big leagues too!" But Lenny never got a chance to catch a ball, he never even had to move his feet out there in centerfield when Doc was pitching.

And it was weird. Doc wasn't but what, seventeen, eighteen years old? And already he had that dangerous moniker, Doctor K. I guess no matter how old you are you are going to scare people if you are striking everybody out. And remember, it was only a year after this that Doc was striking out 276 people in the major leagues. As a pitcher he was already *bad*. Yet here at Tidewater he was also still obviously just a little kid.

I was driving out to the ballpark one day when I first saw him, styling along in this Camaro he had. That was the day he came in, first day any of us had seen him. None of us knew who he was, as yet. On the side of that Camaro, in flashy little letters, it said, "Doctor K." I thought, "What in the world is *that*?" So we get out to the ballpark, and dang if that monogrammed Camaro isn't sitting there in the parking lot. "I've got to go get *on* somebody about this," I said. But when we got into the clubhouse and met Doc, we saw right away he was just a very nice, very mellow young kid who at that point was in way over his head. He looked like a fish out of water, acting real subdued and a little scared.

I kind of took him under my wing. It was a rainy day. I took him out and we did our running together in the rain. The kid had got to a high level of baseball so fast he had no idea what to expect. As we were running along, I tried to tell him a few little things about where to go and what to do, who to be with, what to expect — sharing my veteran's wisdom, you know.

Well, the way I figure it I must have talked to Doc pretty good, because it didn't take him long to get his feet on the ground. The next year, while I was still slaving away down there in Triple-A, that kid was up in the big leagues, just *dominating* people.

Already there at Tidewater you could see great things coming. Doc had a great fastball, for one thing. For two, at this time he still had an impossible-to-hit breaking ball. And he was even experimenting with throwing some change-ups. He was just *killing* those hitters, they didn't even stand a chance. I didn't have to see much of that to know he was soon going to be heading up. Seeing that kind of thing, you know what you're seeing is once in a lifetime.

Payback

We had a pretty nice little team at Tidewater that year. We had Clint Hurdle and Gary Rajsich and Ron Gardenhire. We had Wally Backman, Rick Anderson, Ronn Reynolds. I think John Gibbons was there. Good players, and a very good team. We got into the Triple-A World Series against Portland. We beat them, and I got my Triple-A World Series ring, which I wore around for years afterward.

In fact for a while there I was in the running for Most Valuable Player in that little World Series. I threw five perfect innings of relief in one game, and then did another relief job where I was also shutting them down pretty hard. But Gary Rajsich hit about .400, with a couple of three-run dingers, and they gave him the MVP over me. It was a big old motorcycle they were giving away. I kind of liked the looks of that thing, to tell you the truth, I really had my eye on it. I love motorcycles. And here the guy who wins it is Gary, who can't even drive one. Well, Wally Backman jumped on it and got Gary up on the back and they went spinning around the infield and all around the field. That big hog stirred up some dust and noise. In fact when Wally got off, he looked a little spooked by the ride. "That thing's got *way* more power than you are ever gonna need," he said.

And so who should be playing for Portland in that series, and coming up to hit against me, but Luis Aguayo, the same guy whose triple a year earlier had ruined my chance for a no-hitter. I looked up and thought, "Wait a second, I know him. Well, I'll get back on top of him this time." It was definitely in the back of my mind, that little bit of payback, when I saw him standing up there. Nothing personal, but the guy had taken my one big shot away from me. I punched him out on four pitches.

You're Going to Get Killed

I figured somebody must have been paying attention to how well I did in that '83 Triple-A World Series, because about a week after it was over the Cubs made a trade to pick me up. The Mets got a couple of young arms out of the deal. Neither one of those guys they got for me ever made it to the big leagues; by a roundabout route I was back in the Mets system eight months later.

At that time I was encouraged that Chicago seemed to want me. I say "seemed," because of the way things turned out. In September of '83 when the Cubs traded for me they were finishing out the season under an interim manager, Charlie Fox. After going home and then on down to pitch a little winter ball in Puerto Rico, where as it turned out I did a lot more hanging out on the beach than pitching, I got to Arizona in the spring and found out they had a new manager, Jim Frey. That turned out to be bad news for me, because Jim Frey didn't care for the way I pitched.

Well, that was a tough one. Before going out there, I'd thought I had a great shot to make the Chicago club. I thought it was going to be a real opportunity. But as soon as Jim Frey saw me throw, he got busy trying to change me around. To start with, he wanted me to pitch all lefties the same way, on the outside part of the plate. I wanted to come inside on them, too, every now and then, if I could. "If you come inside to left-handed hitters, you're going to get killed," Jim said. "They will be coming out of their shoes every time you throw the ball."

The next thing I knew, my whole way of doing things was getting rebuilt from the ground up. In my first five minutes of throwing on the side down there in Arizona, they had me doing five different things I'd never done before. They tried to tinker with my submarine style. They wanted me to change my release point, to do things more like Dan Quisenberry, the sidearmer who was having such a great run with Kansas City at that time. "That's not my way,"

I said. "He gets his effects his way, I get mine my way. I feel like I've been doing fine." To me it was a case of, It's not broken, don't try to fix it. My way of doing things had been working just fine for me at the end of last season when they traded for me, why was it suddenly no good now in the spring?

In the Cactus League that spring I got in exactly three innings of work. I gave up a home run, which in Arizona is not that hard to do. Anybody will tell you, in that light air one dinger is no big deal. Aside from that it was three punch-outs, three pop-ups, three weak little groundballs. So three innings, one hit, one run. That was all the work Jim Frey was going to give me. If I wasn't going to change for them, the Cubs weren't going to pitch me. You can guess who won that little battle of wills.

In one game I did get into, I was supposed to be going two or three innings. Now, the Cubs had not yet won a spring training game to that point — I think they only won two or three that whole spring. In my first inning I did just fine, three-up, three-down. We came up to bat, got a couple guys on and it was my turn to hit. Now this was only the fifth inning, spring training game, no big deal. I was looking for a bat, but they told me to sit back down. They were sending up a pinch hitter! I went back and sat down on the bench next to Larry Bowa. I was just shaking my head — I'd been throwing real well, and now this. Larry just looked right at me and said, "I guess they aren't used to anyone doing that well."

That was my last appearance as a Cub. They cut me and sent me over to the minor league camp. Then on the last day of camp they traded me back over to the Braves for a left-hander, Ron Meredith. He never did much for them, but at that point getting back what I was worth probably didn't matter as much to the Cubs as just getting rid of me.

Released Again

By that time the '84 big league season was a week old, so the Atlanta pitching staff was already pretty much set. The Braves shipped me straight down to their Triple-A team in Richmond, where I'd pitched so well five years earlier. This time around I didn't do well there at all.

The problem was, I wasn't getting to pitch enough. I'd had very little work all spring in Arizona, and now at Richmond they were only using me to face a hitter here, a hitter there. That wasn't doing me any good. To be effective I've always needed a lot of work. I'd been there about five or six weeks, and had thrown only about fifteen innings, when the blade fell.

My e.r.a. at the time was up near double figures, but as it turned out, the fact that I was getting lit up a little bit by those Triple-A hitters was only part of the reason Atlanta was letting me go. There was a bottom-line explanation, I later found out. The story I got was that Ted Turner was in a little bit of a tight spot financially, and had had his comptroller sit down and go over the Richmond box scores. That guy noticed I'd had a bad game. He looked up my salary, saw that I had a major league contract and was making forty thousand dollars. He reported back to the boss, and I got my release from the Braves a couple of days later.

When you get released, it's always scary. You never know how long you're going to be out of work. That's not a situation anyone likes to be in. You realize everything can be taken away from you at any moment. That realization can be real unsettling. Having been there before never really makes it easier to get through those times.

The strange thing is the guy who had to tell me I was released by the Braves this time was the same guy who had done it four years earlier, Eddie Haas. Eddie had managed me at Savannah and now he was managing me here at Richmond. If he hadn't enjoyed releasing me before, I could tell he hated doing it this time. In fact, I *know* he did, because after that he was always going out of his way to try to help me any time he could.

In '91 when I was with the Twins, I was living in a hotel up there in Minnesota. One day I ran into Eddie, who was then scouting for Montreal. He was staying at that hotel. We sat down and talked, and I told him I didn't know if the Twins planned on keeping me around. We were in the World Series that year, and after the Series was over, sure enough, I found myself out of work again. When Eddie heard the news, he pushed Montreal to offer me a contract. And as a matter of fact they did. And I had a wonderful spring training with them, but then got cut.

That made three times I'd been released in my career, and Eddie Haas was involved with all three of them. Every ballplayer who's ever played the game is at least a little bit superstitious. I'm forty-five years old right now, but I'm still not totally convinced I couldn't come back out and pitch in the major leagues tomorrow. I've always got my eye out for a job opening. Just don't get Eddie Haas mixed up in it. Eddie was the nicest Grim Reaper I ever met.

I Need to Throw

So in May of '84 I ended up back at Tidewater. Dave Rosenfield, the general manager over there, had always liked me. As soon as he heard that I'd been released, Rosie was calling over to Richmond trying to find me. He said I should come on over and throw. They just wanted to make sure that my arm was all right, that I wasn't hurt or anything. My old history of arm trouble always haunted me. So I went on over to Norfolk. Bob Schaeffer was the Tidewater manager at that point, Al Jackson was the pitching coach. They had me throw on the side, checked me out. After they watched me for about five minutes, they said, "There ain't nothing wrong with him, he's fine." I told them the only thing wrong with me was that I hadn't been getting enough work. "You all know I need to throw." They knew me, that the more I threw the better I got, whereas if I didn't work very much I just wasn't effective.

We went on up to Maine and played the Cleveland Triple-A team in their park at Old Orchard Beach. We were just getting beat to death, and I was getting hit *hard*. Schaeffer came strolling out to the mound and said, "Listen, I'm just going to leave you out here. You can use the work." I told him, "Fine." That was a kind of turning-point for my season. I could have gotten killed out there, the way Jim Frey had predicted a couple of months earlier. And I sure was going to be running up some seriously bad stats unless I kicked in right then. Well, I kicked in. Just getting to stay out there and work a little extra when I was struggling was the thing that allowed me to pick myself up and turn my season around.

I went on and I really picked up after that. Instead of getting myself killed, I went on a big long roll of shutout innings, and wound up winning ten games at Tidewater that year. Statistically it was the best year I'd had in professional baseball up to that time — 10-2, 1.90 e.r.a.

I'm Not Here as a Coach

That good year at Tidewater got me invited back in the spring of '85. When I got to spring training the main thing I saw was that the Mets were trying to push their younger pitchers up to the big leagues. The young guys were the priority, and I was kind of stuck on a side track. This was getting to be a routine thing for me by now, in fact I was getting used to it. They wanted me to be helping them coach the guys who were going to be coming on and passing me over. That was a new twist.

I got cut on the last day of spring training. (That made twice, the same thing had happened in '82.) They asked me to stay behind in camp with the Triple-A team and help instruct the young pitchers. And I'm thinking, "Now wait a minute, here. I'm still trying to make it to the big leagues. I'm not here as a coach."

Chris and I had got married that spring down in St. Pete, and we had her two kids with us, so in my new position as family man I was not about to give up on shooting for a steady big league job just yet.

Then when the season got going they sent a couple of those young guys up to the major league club ahead of me. Those guys had trouble, got hit, got sent down, then got brought back up again. They'd get hit around again, here they'd come back down. All through this time I'm pitching really well down there in Triple-A. Forty-five innings. Earned run average down around one. I was saying, "Hey, how long is it going to be before I get my shot?"

I Survived the Amazing Fourth of July Game

I did get to go back up to New York for the second half of that '85 season. They were in a little bit of a pennant drive up there, contending against the Cardinals, so it was a pretty exciting time to get to go up. I remember I was one of the two oldest guys on the Tidewater team at the time I got the call — me and Ed Glynn, the Flushing Flash. Ed was thirty-two, I was thirty-one. Ed had been with four different organizations and kicked around a lot, so he could understand what this meant to me. He was just ecstatic when he heard I was going up. I think he got just about as excited as I did. Maybe it represented a kind of symbolic victory for us old guys, in his mind.

For an old guy I didn't pitch half badly in the big leagues once I got back up. Davey Johnson said he liked having me around, and I think I did prove myself useful. "The insurance policy," Davey would call me. They could count on me when any kind of trouble came up. Davey ended up using me every which way that season. I worked middle relief, long relief — *early* relief, I preferred to call it — but I also came on late a time or two and picked myself up a save, and even stepped in four times as a rescue starter. I came up June 21 and got into twenty-two big league games, threw fifty-six innings, went 3-4 with a real good e.r.a., a couple of points down under three.

I wasn't back up in New York long before I found myself thrown into some real wild games, right in the thick of the pennant race. The craziest might have been a game in Atlanta against the Braves on the fourth of July. The Braves were going nowhere that year under my old friend, Eddie Haas, but they battled us in that holiday game like there was no tomorrow. In fact there almost was no tomorrow, because that game ran on so long it nearly swallowed up July fifth as well.

I've still got a button that says I SURVIVED THE 4TH OF JULY GAME. I pitched in the game. For that matter, I was in line to get the win during that game, if it had come to a nice quiet ending like it was supposed to. I came in early and went about three innings. By the time I left we had a three or four run lead. I was just cruising along fine, but Davey yanked me out of there because he wanted to get Jesse Orosco some work. Jesse hadn't pitched in three or four days. When Davey came out, I handed him the baseball and said, "Okay, that's fine with me. I'm sticking with my W." I went inside to the clubhouse, took a shower, had a little cerveza. Once you're out of the game, you can clean up and sit in there and have a beer. Brent Gaff was in there too. So we're sipping our beers, killing time, and now Jesse starts running into trouble. He was not having a good night at all. All of a sudden the Braves had tied it up.

That game ended up going nineteen innings. Felt more like sixteen weeks, it took so much waiting around to get that thing over. We had people falling down drunk back up there in the clubhouse. Gaffer, he'd been drinking since about the sixth inning. We had two long rain delays. By the middle of the second one he'd passed out. Meanwhile, all this time the caterers kept bringing the post-game food in and then taking it back out. Every time we got what looked like a safe lead, they'd come in and lay out the spread. All of a sudden the game gets tight again, they cover it all up and take it back out. They must have done that four or five times during the course of the night.

The game went on until four o'clock in the morning. We figured at last we had it won when we scored in the top of the seventeenth. But then, dang if in their half the Braves didn't come up off the floor and make another run at us. Now Tom Gorman's in there pitching — Goose Gorefax we used to call him, a mixture of Goose Gossage and Sandy Koufax. The Braves had completely run out of pinch hitters now, and it was the pitcher's turn to bat. Rick Camp came up there. Rick Camp had a lifetime B.A. of about zero-fifty, no home runs. What were the odds he'd do anything other than strike out against Tom Gorman? Obviously Rick Camp had no chance. He was just swinging hard in case one of Goose's fastballs hit his bat. Well, one did. Boom, home run.

Finally it was four o'clock in the morning, maybe about 7,000 people still left in the park. Everybody still hanging there, that game was so weird they just couldn't go home. In the nineteenth inning we took the lead again, 16-13. Then in the Braves' half we had our last available pitcher out there, Ron Darling. Rick Camp came up, couple of guys on base — would you believe Camp hit another long fly? This time the ball went foul. Ron struck him out and saved us from the Twilight Zone. The Atlanta people actually went ahead and shot off the fourth of July fireworks — the whole shebang, even though by now it was almost getting light on the fifth.

What a game that was. You can bet our pitchers gave a little grief to those guys who couldn't hold the lead for us. They were coming back at us, saying, "Well, I've never pitched at four o'clock in the morning before." And our answer came right back, "Well, those guys haven't ever been *hitting* at four o'clock in the morning before, either." I guess with everything that happened in that game, it finally came down to where all the weirdness just kind of equaled out.

A Standing Ovation

All three of my wins in '85 came as a starter. The most enjoyable of those victories came on the twenty-second of August. We were playing the Giants at home. The race was really heating up now, for us every game was important. That night Sid Fernandez was scheduled to make the start, but Sid got sick and didn't tell anybody. He went out to try to get ready to pitch the first inning and couldn't make it. They called on me.

It was a complete surprise. I'd already done my working out, showered, and was just hanging out in the clubhouse, resting. Had done my running, gone through my daily exercise routine — three or four hundred sit-ups, a lot of pushups, and so on. That drill would always leave me pretty well worn-out, and now this was my regular re-charging time. At that point just before a game I could always count on having about fifteen minutes to kill. Don't have to go out to the bullpen yet, don't have to go anywhere or do anything, my time belongs to me. So there I am in my long underwear, no shirt, fiddling with a crossword puzzle. A guy comes running in the clubhouse to get me. "Sid's sick, you've got to go out and pitch the game!" "Are you serious?" *I put my shoe on my head, my shirt down on my foot* — I don't know what all, I just went running out there. Got warmed up in about five minutes. I mean, the adrenalin was flowing so hard, I was warm almost immediately.

And I stayed hot. That night those hitters were dropping like tin soldiers. I don't think I had to throw but 86 or 87 pitches to get through nine innings. I had it all working. Movement, control, everything was just right there for me. That night I loved to pitch. When you're going like that, there's no better feeling in life. It ended up a three-hit shutout. When we were walking off the field after the last out, Ray Knight, who was playing third base, came up next to me and said, "That was the best game I've ever seen pitched." That's coming from a guy who's seen one or two baseball games in his life, so it made me feel pretty good.

My bunting gave me a lot less to brag about than my pitching that night. I'm normally a pretty good bunter. Well, that night I had Vida Blue pitching against me. Vida was bringing it about 95 miles per hour. I mean, Vida threw *hard*. Vida *played* hard, he *laughed* hard, he *smoked cigarettes* hard. What he did, he was deep into doing. When he drank, he drank *scotch*. When he threw, he threw some *serious* fastballs. My first at bat against Vida that night, I struck out on three pitches, bunted right through three high heaters and never touched one of them. Ditto next time up. Six tries, six strikes. That ball was just jumping up on me so quick that for the first time in my life I was just plain *late on bunts*, and couldn't get one down.

My third time up, Vida was out of the game. They asked me to bunt again. Greg Minton was pitching now for the Giants. Greg threw me a fastball. That ball must have been coming in about 85 miles an hour, but after Vida's heater it looked fat as a grapefruit. Boom, no problem, I laid down my bunt and ran it out.

On my way back to the dugout I got a shock. The Shea Stadium crowd was on its feet, giving me a standing ovation. The people were applauding me for finally getting my bunt down, but also for my pitching. On a night of the unexpected, that standing O was the most unexpected thing. Never in my wildest dreams did I dare to imagine getting a curtain call. It was a first. Looking up into all those appreciative faces, all I could say was, "Thank you."

You'd Have to Kill Me First

If that sweet little three-hit shutout stand-in job for Sid in late August had been the last impression I left the Mets with in '85, things might have gone better for me the next year. As it was, after winning three starts I got sent out to pitch a game against the Pirates at a point in September when we were just barely hanging on in the race. I got touched up for five runs in six innings and got beat. We came up three games shy of the Cardinals, so maybe that stretch-run start they'd entrusted me with was affecting their opinion of me a little bit. At any rate it wasn't my shutout but the one game I'd lost that was the last taste I'd left them with, and that piece of bad luck probably didn't help my cause a whole lot.

In '86 the Mets asked me back as a non-roster player. As usual, they protected their younger people on the forty-man roster, because those were the people they didn't want to lose in the draft. Well, I was used to those odds. That winter I went to the Dominican Republic and worked as hard as I could to make a good impression on the people in New York.

I'd been in the Dominican in the winter of '84 and pitched well, so after my '85 season they invited me back. I'd just got married, so Chris came down with me. We got ourselves two rooms, with room service. Still, Chris didn't like it down there. Too much culture shock, I guess. By now I'd learned my little bit of Spanish, but Chris hardly knew a word. We'd go in to some little place to eat, she'd try to order chicken in Spanish. No luck. They'd tell her to speak English. And that hotel about drove her crazy. Every other day the electricity was going out. Ooh, she just hated that. She kind of got a green aura around her down there, where whenever she was around things would break down or screw up. Something was always going wrong.

One time we had an off day, Chris and I were going to drive over to the beach. There was a big resort town over there where we knew some people. We figured we'd go over and hang around a little, swim, eat, kick back. On the way over we stopped to eat a little chicken. Chris swallowed a bone and it got stuck in her throat. I got her over real quick to the team doctor. Would you believe the team doctor was a gynecologist? He wanted to take an x-ray. We were just getting ready to get the x-ray when the electricity went out. He said, "Come back when the electricity goes on." I'd seen that before. Every time you got hurt down there you had to wait for the electricity to go on to get your x-ray, so I was ready for that. But Chris, she wasn't. She was ready to go home from the day she got there.

I had to leave before the playoffs, but for as long as I was down there I was one of the top pitchers. For being pitcher of the month they award you all this stuff, a case of rum in big bottles, a car battery. I gave away a whole lot of rum to the Latin players when I left. Once again, being out of the U. S. was a real learning event for me. I mean, in the Dominican the whole scale of life you'd see around you was nothing like what it is in the United States. There'd be little ladies leading their donkeys up the middle of the street. It was a different world. And then one thing happened that finally brought Chris to the end of her rope.

The team was going out on a road trip. I went down to catch the bus, right on time, but it was already gone. I could not *believe* that, the first time in my baseball life I ever heard of a team bus leaving *early*. "We thought everybody was here so we took off," they said later. So I had to go drive my own car forty-five minutes over to San Pedro de Macoris, the place where all the shortstops come from. On the way back I had three other guys with me, two Americans and one Latin coach. It was late at night. I was doing forty, forty-five miles per hour on the main road from Santo Domingo to Santiago. It's a two-lane road, and even though it's a main highway, the Dominican Highway One, it's in real bad shape, especially on the side of the road that's travelled by a lot of heavily loaded trucks headed to Santiago. That side of the road was all torn up and full of potholes, but the other side was okay, so everybody just went ahead and drove on the wrong side of the road. And then, down there they don't dim their headlights. They don't believe in it. Either they drive with no lights on at all, or they drive with their brights. So I'm going along, I see this car coming straight at me. I'm half-blinded in the bright lights, but I manage to get around it. I'm in this little Japanese sub-compact car. All of a sudden there's a tremendous impact. There'd been a horse standing there, and I hadn't even seen it. I hit that horse. It went right into my front windshield and shattered the glass. We had glass in our faces, blood all over the place. Now I'm in the middle of nowhere with a dead horse, a wrecked car. We had to go to the police.

All this time Chris was back in our hotel waiting for me. I came bouncing in at two o'clock in the morning with blood all over me and this story about a dead horse. She said, "That's it, I'm gonna leave." By this time she'd already been down there a good bit, and her grandmother was sick back home. She packed up and left. I just said, That's it, culture.

Came back from the Dominican with a 5-1, 1.93 record, feeling pretty good about my chances. But then when I got to camp things immediately started looking a lot tougher. They had traded for Bobby Ojeda, and a couple of other guys were coming back from injuries. I could see that I represented the insurance policy, again. If other people stayed healthy, I'd be gone.

At this point I had one year and sixty-six days of big league service time to show for my ten years in professional baseball. I had a family, I wanted to buy a house. I had to be thinking about my future. I could have considered walking away from baseball, but I never did. You'd have had to kill me first. I just kept figuring if I could get up and stay up one whole year and finally get myself established, all my work would be worth the trouble — because once I was established I *knew* I could pitch well enough to stay around for a while.

Some Celebration

They cut me and I didn't kick up a fuss, just packed my bags and went on down to Norfolk to try to put some numbers up and be ready when the Mets called. I told them I'd be on the beach at Tidewater, they'd know where to find me. I definitely thought I'd pitched well enough in the spring to make the team out of camp, and I still think so to this day. But I followed orders. I went on down and did the Tidewater shuffle — got down there in time to make the start for the Tides on opening night.

Back up in New York, two weeks into the season Ed Lynch tore up some cartilage in his knee and the call went out for the insurance policy. I was brought back up. For the next five weeks or so I had a pretty nice little ride, working a half dozen times out of the bullpen with a 2.70 e.r.a. Things were looking good enough that I decided to bring Chris along on a West Coast trip we were making toward the end of May. It was her birthday coming up, and to celebrate we were going to make that little trip together.

When we were in Los Angeles, I started to get a funny feeling because of something that happened down in the bullpen. Rick Aguilera and I were down there. At that point Rick had lost his spot in the rotation and there was talk going around that he might be shipped out to Tidewater to get in some work. But here in this game they got Rick up to throw in the early innings. Then he sat back down. After a while the bullpen phone rang again. It was the sixth inning now, my time of the game to come in. I started to take off my jacket to warm up, but they told me to sit back down. The call was for Roger McDowell. Now Roger McDowell was a late inning man, this definitely wasn't his normal role. It was my role. It looked to me at that moment like my job might have just evaporated.

We went on up to San Francisco. When we got there, who should show up in the hotel but Doug Sisk. The last anybody knew, Doug Sisk was down at Tidewater. He'd been farmed out. When we saw Dougie in the hotel, we all knew something was up. If Doug Sisk was back on the roster, either Rick Aguilera was going to take the hit, or I was.

We had an open date on a Monday, and that night Chris and I went out to dinner to celebrate her birthday. Ron Darling and his wife Toni were going out for the evening with us. We were all on our way out of the hotel, getting ready to have a party, when I got pulled over by Arthur Richman, a very fine gentleman, the traveling secretary of the team. He told me I should get packed up. Neither Davey Johnson, the manager, nor Frank Cashen, the general manager, were around to talk to me, nor was Joe McIlvaine, the vice president of baseball affairs. Finally I got in touch with another vice president, Al Harazin. He was nice, but it wasn't his department. There was nobody to discuss things with. I was Tidewater-bound.

We went out and celebrated Chris's birthday that night anyway. Some celebration. Well, it was okay, we swallowed back our disappointment and had ourselves a good time. Then we went back to the hotel and got packed in a big hurry for our flight to the East Coast.

I knew I hadn't pitched badly, but I wasn't going to whine and complain. What was I going to say — I'd held up my end and they'd let me down again? That thought ran through my mind but I kept it to myself. The Mets might have been thinking along the same lines. A day or two after I got back to Norfolk, the Mets publicist called up to the Tides' clubhouse, from San Diego. Frank Cashen wanted to make sure I'd reported. They didn't want to lose track of their insurance policy.

The Ring I Almost Got

At the end of the Triple-A season in September I was due to be recalled. I'd had a real good year at Tidewater, pitching in every different kind of role — long man, short man, closer, starter. Had four wins, seven saves, a complete game, a 2.41 e.r.a. in eighty innings down there. Bob Schaeffer was still managing the Tides, and now John Cumberland was the pitching coach. They kept encouraging me to work hard and pushing to get me brought back up, telling the people upstairs I was doing a better job than anybody else they had down there. By that time the Mets were running away with their division and headed for what promised to be a great post season, so I was dying to get back up, but nobody had given me the word.

I pitched the next-to-last game of the Triple-A season for Tidewater. The Tides needed to win one of those last two games to get into the playoffs. Two of their starting pitchers were hurt, so they asked me to make the start. I figured I had no place to go, and I'm always ready for anything.

Now I hadn't had an at-bat all season, but in that game, as fate would have it, I had to come up and hit. I'd set down the first six batters I'd faced and was feeling pretty good about things by the time it came to my turn to step up there. I was going to stand in and try to do my best, because we needed to win that game. I drew a walk, and then with two out Stanley Jefferson drove a ball out between the outfielders. I made up my mind right then and there to try to score from first. I thought the third base coach, Sam Perlozzo, would probably hold me at third, but he surprised me and sent me. Well, we needed that run. I came barreling around third in high gear and started bearing down on home plate. At that point I saw I had a little problem. The catcher was standing there with the ball, blocking the plate. I figured if I tried a last-minute slide, I'd slam into his shinguards and break my leg. So I decided to try the old gung-ho maneuver and dive over him. That was bad decision number two.

The impact of the collision knocked me up in the air and I landed on home plate right on my pitching shoulder. Next thing that happened, I was standing in front of an x-ray machine, holding a five-pound weight while they took a picture of the gap I'd just created in my shoulder. I'd dislocated *and* separated it, the team doctor told me. Then he hit me with some news that was even worse. "I heard you were supposed to be going back up to New York the day after tomorrow," he said. "Oh man," I said, "I wish somebody had told me that about three hours ago, before I got talked into going out and pitching that game!"

The Mets, as most everybody knows, went on and beat Houston in the league playoffs and then beat Boston in the World Series. I wouldn't have been eligible to play but I'd at least have been traveling with the team and sitting on the bench with them, if I hadn't been hurt. And then, I didn't get a World Series ring. The organization made the decision on who'd get rings. It came down to a judgment call, and it was decided I hadn't contributed enough. There was a little bit of inequity there. Ed Lynch, who'd pitched one inning in the regular season and then got hurt, and then when he could pitch again was traded to the Cubs — Ed got a ring. (One little irony there was the fact that Ed had got hurt in the fifth game of the season, and the guy who'd come up to fill his spot for a week was me.) And there were several of us who'd played more than Ed Lynch, yet had not gotten rings. Since they'd given rings to people all through the organization, from the trainers all the way down to Single-A, the secretaries and office people, just about everybody, those of us who'd played a little and didn't get one, we just didn't understand.

Now when the players on the team came to dividing up shares of the World Series prize money at the end of the year, it was a different story altogether. The players voted me a quarter share, and that turned out to be worth $25,000. The players thought it was fair to cut me in, but the organization, which was making the decision on the rings, just didn't see it the same way. It took me almost ten years to collect that ring. This wasn't just a small thing to me, either. Anybody who's seen a major league World Series ring will understand why. We're talking about a big heavy ring here, with a lot of diamonds in it. Those rings are so heavy you have to take them off when you're driving any distance at all, because they'll put your hands to sleep.

The way it happened was pretty funny. Ed Lynch went on after his playing career to be an assistant general manager with the Mets and then later became general manager in Chicago. In 1995 the Cubs came in to play the Mets one time, and somebody in the Mets' office decided to mess with Ed a little bit by having a trivia question put up on the scoreboard: "Name the 1986 Met pitcher who worked only one inning in the regular season, yet was awarded a World Series ring." Randy Myers, who by then had gone over to play with the Cubs, was sitting out in the bullpen. Randy looked up and saw that sign on the scoreboard. Randy had got in just about as many innings in '86 as I had, maybe ten, and he also hadn't got a ring. It was still a sore point with him. When Randy saw the trivia question go up there, the whole ring business ticked him off all over again, and this time he just about went ballistic.

Next day he stormed up into the Mets' office and demanded those rings for us. Joe McIlvaine, the vice president of the team, was up there. Joe agreed to ask the company to re-open the mold and make more rings. The company said all right. But Randy was going to have to pay for it, and the prices had gone up. Randy said that was okay, he'd buy rings for all of us. But in the meantime, Mr. Wilpon, the owner of the Mets, came into this. I guess Randy had embarrassed him a little. Mr. Wilpon finally put in the cost of the original rings, Randy chipped in the balance, and those of us who were cheated out of them back then have now got our '86 World Series rings at last.

What I Missed

That fall I had to look at the post-season games I'd missed out on by tuning in from a greater distance than I would have liked. Chris and I were in Seminole, Florida. We had moved into a little apartment until we could find a house. We watched the playoffs and World Series on TV. What a great stretch of games it was, what a wonderful run. I remember sitting there in front of the TV, screaming and yelling. Chris would have already gone off to bed, and I'd be up jumping around and dancing and cheering my ex-teammates on.

In fact, we'd been following the Mets all season on television when I was at Tidewater. If I was pitching a game for the Tides, Chris would tape the Mets game from WOR. Then when I got home and we were eating supper, we'd turn on the VCR and see how the Mets were doing. One game I remember we were getting real involved in, it was a real tense game against the Reds, we were getting completely into it and then all of a sudden the tape ran out. We had to wait until the next day to find out Hojo had hit a late home run to win it. That game we missed the climax of was kind of representative of the whole '86 season for me — a kind of bitter-sweet year, memorable mostly for what I missed out on.

Bad Penny

After missing that chance in '86, I really wanted to make amends. That winter I pushed myself harder than I ever had in my life. In September of '86 I had a bump the size of a walnut on my right collarbone and couldn't *pick up* a baseball, let alone throw one. I rehabbed that injury all winter. Worked out on my own money and time at the Mets training center in St. Petersburg, every day for the next five-and-a-half months. I wore the toe clean off a baseball shoe, I worked so hard. Kept plugging away, and finally I got my shoulder healed up to where I was ready to go out and pitch my very best in spring training, 1987.

I had pitched five scoreless innings of two-hit ball in four relief appearances that spring when Davey Johnson called me into his office and told me the numbers were bad and I was getting cut back again. Well, that about tore it. I'd done so well, and now they'd taken away my shot. Oh, I was hot. I cursed my way out of Davey's office. After all those years of hearing about the numbers game, I was tired of it. I did some venting. "Some day it's got to be *my* number!" Slammed the door behind me. Who happens to be standing there in the clubhouse when I walk out but Frank Cashen. I started to cool down a little bit, when I saw Frank. "Don't worry, Leachie," he said. "You'll always keep showing back up around here. You're like a bad penny."

A lot of people who were used to my easygoing ways were pretty surprised by my blowing up like that. I'd been overlooked so long, I guess I couldn't take it when it happened one more time. I had watched too many guys step over me, for too many years. I knew I could be an effective major league pitcher. I was having my best spring and it didn't seem to matter.

Maybe all that disappointment was a test. I don't know, but how it turned out was, a few days later the news came down that Roger McDowell had to have a hernia operation, and Doc Gooden was going on the disabled list to check into a drug clinic. The numbers changed. About three days before camp broke, here came the call to the Tidewater club for their insurance policy, and almost before they'd had a chance to miss me I turned back up with the major league team, this time to stay.

Part Seven
Unlikely Hero

Opening Day, 1987

Though I'd been in seventy big league games, it was the first time I'd ever been there when they introduced the team on the first day of the season. Everybody goes out on the field and stands in a line. You've got a big crowd out there at Shea — opening day for a world champion team, coming off a season when they won 108 games. The loudspeaker announced "Number 26, Terry Leach, pitcher." You'd have to be a cold-blooded person not to feel a little chill down your spine, at a moment like that.

That same day they gave out the World Series rings. Even though I didn't get one, it was neat just being there, watching the little ceremony and sharing all that joy. I remember Keith Hernandez, one guy I really liked a lot, being so happy to get that ring that he just popped it on his finger right there and then, grinning and showing it off to everybody. That was definitely a special moment. The more I saw of those other guys' rings being flashed around, the more fired-up I was starting to feel about going out and earning one of my own.

The Baseball Gods

Nineteen eighty seven turned out to be a year of struggle and trial for the Mets as a team. They started out the season with just an unbelievable string of injuries to the pitching staff. One old baseball rule is, When you're coming into the season as top dog, everybody's going to be gunning for you. I remember that first month, when we were scuffling a little, Mike Schmidt made some comments about how the Mets were carrying themselves in a kind of cocky way that had everybody in baseball out to get them. If the Mets won again, they were going to go down as one of the greatest teams in the history of baseball. "There's something about the baseball gods," Mike Schmidt said. "Believe me, they're out there. And staying in the good graces of the baseball gods is something the Mets aren't particularly good at."

A Blessed Year

Maybe the Mets did have the baseball gods against them that season. But that turned out to be a kind of backward blessing for me, because I finally got the chance to pitch I'd always prayed for. And that turned out to be just a blessed year for me.

I wasn't suffering under any illusions. I knew I was only with the team on Opening Day because Doc Gooden and Roger McDowell were absent. I was preying on the jobs of guys who were down. It was like being a vulture. Well, I wasn't going to waste time feeling sorry about it. I told Davey Johnson I understood certain guys were just getting a chance because we'd suddenly come up short of pitchers, but that at the same time I wasn't going to settle for just being temporary help any more. I intended to stay. Let someone else be the insurance policy.

One thing led to another. The first couple of months pitchers just kept going down. Every time somebody got healed up and was about to come back, I'd be about to get sent down. But then somebody else would get hurt, so they'd hang on to me.

Pretty soon Davey got to giving me the ball more and more. It was our old thing — he knew me, he said I liked to be abused. I was hot. I was on. Everything I threw was perfect. I didn't have to put much thought into it, I just did it. It was a wonderful thing — the best extended stretch of pitching I'd ever done in my life.

I worked early relief in April and May, but then toward the end of May the injury situation got so bad that they were in danger of running out of starting pitchers. I remember one night after I'd pitched a couple of scoreless innings in a game, Wally Backman was standing next to me, shaving. "Leachie," he said, "we're going to have to throw you out there to start one time. Every time we put you out there in the middle of a game you throw a gem. We've got to get you out there at the beginning!"

We went out West, and our starting pitchers were dropping like flies. On top of Doc being still missing, now Bobby Ojeda was out for the season. In San Francisco David Cone was trying to bunt and took a fastball off the pinky of his pitching hand, had to have a pin put in his finger. The next day Rick Aguilera went down with an elbow ligament sprain.

We were headed down to L.A. Davey had pitched me five out of the six days. He gave me two days off, then threw me in to make a start in Dodger Stadium against Fernando Valenzuela. Fernando was one of the top pitchers in the league right then, but that one night, he was only the second-best starting pitcher in Chavez Ravine. I went six innings, gave up four hits, no earned runs, left with a 5-1 lead. We won it 5-2, I got the win. I bailed them out, that night. It was a point in the season where, though it was still early, people were wondering if the Mets could even hang on in the race. I'd gone out and held their season together that night.

That was the game that really gave me some momentum. Afterwards Davey told the reporters I had a lot of guts, a lot of heart. He knew me, he was ready to give me credit. The Dodgers' manager, Tommy Lasorda, on the other hand, was a little bit grudging. He said something about how his hitters had made me look like Walter Johnson. Tommy was just ticked off because an unknown guy had beaten his ace.

Unlikely Hero

Newspaper guys were waiting around the clubhouse that night to interview me, I later heard. Well, that had never happened to me before. I had some friends in the ballpark for the game, and after it was over, I just went off with them. The writers hung out expecting me, but I never came back.

That was the first of June. It was my fourth win of the season, with no losses. I was on my way to winning ten straight games to start that season. The unlikely hero was going to make his little splash. Davey didn't put me into the starting rotation right away. He said I was more valuable to him coming out of the bullpen, because he could go to me time and time again. Some writers called me at the hotel in Los Angeles and asked me what I thought about that. I told them it was fine with me, I liked my role. Between you and me, starting sounded nicer. But I'd never done it steady enough to know if I could do it for a whole season. Trying to go all the way every day takes a lot of endurance, and I had to be honest with myself and admit I didn't really know if I was that strong.

After the win over Fernando in L. A. on the first of June, I went back to the bullpen and pitched relief for the next couple of weeks. Keith Hernandez was starting to call me "Jack," for Jack-of-all-trades. Jesse Orosco and I were the only two guys on the staff who were pitching effectively at that point, so they just kept using us. We were both working nearly every day, but because I worked early and Jesse worked late, I was getting a lot more innings. People were saying I had a bionic arm, I had the best arm God put on a man, to be able to throw as much as I was and thrive on it.

The 16th of the month they came up an arm short again, so I got sent out to start a game in Montreal. The Expos were contending with the Cardinals and us in the East. That team could generate some offense. They had good hitters, and they had Tim Raines, guys who could really run. I knew the first thing I had to try to do was keep those guys off the bases. Okay, I went right after them, no walks, shut them out through eight innings. Got eleven guys on groundballs, because I had that old side-winding sinker of mine working fine. Down the home stretch of that game I retired seventeen batters in a row before they finally scored a couple of runs off me in the ninth. McDowell came in and finished up for me. We won 7-3. I really wanted that shutout. I was getting hungry — pitching very well was just whetting my appetite to do even better.

Now I got to have my little Cinderella tour in the starting rotation. I won my sixth straight in Philadelphia on June 27, then on July 2 in Cincinnati I pitched probably the best game of my whole streak. The Reds were one of the toughest teams in the West. They had some heavy guns, Eric Davis, Dave Parker, serious major league hitters. But not too much was going to intimidate me at that point. I got my shutout that night, a two-hitter. Shut those hot-hitting Reds *down*. That was the third and last shutout of my big league career. I was pitching as effectively as I'd ever pitched in my life. I felt so good out there, it was like I was being gifted.

I think other people could feel it too. I had something special going on. My stuff was just unhittable. In fact, about the sixth inning of that game, as we came running off the field, Keith Hernandez, our first baseman, ran up beside me. "Boy, am I glad I'm not hitting against you," he said. For Mex to be saying that to me just bowled me over. That was coming from a man who could hit *anything*. Remember I told you about what Ray Knight said to me after that game I'd pitched against Vida Blue in '85. Well, this little thing Mex said was the *second* great compliment I'd ever got from a teammate when I was pitching. What was different this time was, I was getting it from a hitter's perspective.

All Good Things Must End

We went down to Atlanta, where I beat the Braves, to stretch my winning streak to eight in a row. As good as it felt to win, that game had a worrisome side to it, because by that time I was pitching in some pain. I had succumbed to the injury bug. The trouble started with my knee, not my arm. On our first trip into Houston earlier that year I'd popped a little bit of cartilage. I hadn't been paying too much attention to it, but during the game in Atlanta that knee really got to hurting. We went on down to Houston, and it got worse. I guess all good things must end sometime: the baseball gods had given me about as much of a run as I was going to get.

Maybe I should have gone on the DL a lot sooner, only I was winning, and I just couldn't quit. I felt like the good Lord was letting me have my little fling, I wanted to see it through. I tried to pitch through the pain but it got worse and worse. Pretty soon things got to where I couldn't push off any more when I was pitching. Then when I got back home at the All-Star break I found I couldn't get in and out of my car. I had to pick my leg up with my hands to move it.

There's that old saying, Once your legs go, your arm goes. It's a very true saying. People suppose that you throw a baseball with your arm, but you don't. You actually throw a baseball with your whole body. You use your legs to generate your velocity. When your legs quit working and you try to make your arm take over, you won't last very long. That's what I tried to do, and that's what happened to me.

I lost all my velocity. Finally it got to where I'll bet you I wasn't throwing 77 miles an hour. I was having a hard time even getting the ball to go over the plate. I'd have to stay inside on the right-handed hitters. For me to bring the ball outside on them for even one pitch, that would take the energy of throwing five pitches. Just to pull that pitch out there real hard, it was a serious chore.

This wasn't working. I had to tell Davey I didn't think I could go any more. We were at the point where use was turning to abuse. He put me on the disabled list for fifteen days, to rest me up.

Davey was managing the National League All-Stars that year, and so he was picking the All-Star pitching staff. I was 8-0 at that point, but of course he knew I was hurting and he wanted to give me that time off. My one chance in my life to be an All-Star, and I had to miss it. The game was out in Oakland. My agent went out there for it. Later on he asked me if I'd hired a couple of people to be there. I said, "No, why?" He said there were these two guys walking around the Oakland Coliseum with a big sign the size of a bedsheet. That sign said, "WHERE THE HELL IS LEACH?"

After the break I came back, but I wasn't the same. Still, I did get to start a few more games. The first day they activated me, they pitched me in relief in St. Louis. Then we went on up to Montreal, and I started against the Expos. I guess I really had that team's number, because I beat them again that night, and then beat them a third time two weeks later back home at Shea.

I stood 10-0 at that point, one beautiful line of black ink in that morning paper. I could treasure my good luck all the more because I knew it wasn't going to last much longer. We went out to Chicago and on the 15th of August my run came to an end with a 7-3 loss to the Cubs. By that time I was almost relieved the undefeated streak was over, because I was pretty wobbly out there. I was hurting and about worn out.

After the loss to the Cubs, Davey put me back in the bullpen. He told me to stop throwing between games. "If I warm you up, you're going in," he told me. "That's the *only* time you're going to be throwing." No more abusing now — the idea was, I'd give my arm a little rest. I'd work out on the stationary bike, get my knee to feeling better. My arm would get the benefit. Constant use had just worn it out.

Cutting back on my throwing like that seemed to work. At any rate I made it to the end of the season somehow. Frankly I probably shouldn't have been playing at all, but we were still in contention. I was needed. Even when I was back in the bullpen, I didn't know but what I might have to come out and pitch a substantial part of the game on any given night. One day we were out in San Francisco, you know how cold it gets there, and they threw me in as a first-inning emergency replacement for Sid Fernandez. I had fifteen minutes to get ready — my old familiar insurance policy role.

Well, as I say, I hung in there and lasted out that year on a wing and a prayer. I finished up 11-1. We came in second, three games back of St. Louis. Somebody asked Wally Backman where the Mets would have been without me. "Twelve games out," Wally said. As soon as the season was over I went in and had my knee operated on and they picked out a lot of that torn-up cartilage. Those bits and pieces, not a ring, were what I had to show for the '87 campaign.

In the Moment

Despite the problems that I ran into with injuries, I've got no complaint about how things turned out for me that year. The good Lord has his reasons for doing things. I'd had a wonderful season, when all was said and done. I'd been given my little fling, and I'd enjoyed just about every minute of it.

When you get hot and have a streak like I did that season you go on and remember little things about it all your life. What I remember best is how absorbed I was in what I was doing, when I was pitching at my peak. I had total concentration. I'd come in after pitching an inning and sit down in the dugout and somebody would say, "What did you throw to so-and-so?" And I'd say, "Did *he* hit?" Because when I was out there during that streak, I was at a point where I neither knew nor cared who was hitting against me. I didn't *like* knowing. I didn't want to be paying attention to that. I wanted those hitters to be attending to *me*.

Of course, I was at a point in my career where I could recognize every hitter. I knew them, yet then again, I didn't want to let my knowing who they were affect the way I pitched to them. I didn't want to let their particular strengths force me into pitching defensively and trying to be too fine. I was throwing well enough that I didn't want to have to change the way I was pitching for anybody. I would pitch to each hitter a certain way, but it would be my way. Some people have books and stuff, they take notes on how they do things, but I never did keep up. I would judge it *that day* — not by anything that had happened in the past but by how I was pitching *that* day, and how each guy was swinging the bat. It was all right there for me in the moment.

Still Learning

The other interesting thing for me about that '87 season was finding out I could still be learning quite a bit about my trade of pitching, despite my gray hairs.

That year I learned how to pitch to left-handed hitters. Before that year, I'd never seen too many of them, to tell you the truth. It had been a rap against me all through my career. That reputation went all the way back to the minor leagues, where I was always getting left behind because supposedly I couldn't get left-handers out. Even in Double-A, I remember a game I started for the Braves' team down in Savannah, the Detroit farm team in Montgomery came out and put up seven left-handed hitters against me. I pitched a complete game and won. So when people said I couldn't handle left-handers, the truth was I'd just never been given that much of a chance.

That season, when I got thrown into the starting rotation, I could see I was going to *have* to get left-handers out. I worked on that with Vern Hoscheit, the Mets' bullpen coach, and the pitching coach, Mel Stottlemyre. Before that year, when I was pitching against left-handers I'd pretty much always stayed on the outside of the plate. I remember when I was with Chicago that one spring, Jim Frey had insisted I pitch left-handers *away, away, away*. "Never come inside on them," Jim said. But now here Vern and Mel were showing me that if I never came inside on left-handers, those guys were going to be able to lean out over the plate and rake my outside pitches. They had *no fear*, and they could go leaning out there and do some damage.

So I took that advice. I started to pitch inside against left-handers a little bit more. And the more left-handers I saw, the better I got at pitching to them. I figured out exactly where to set my release point, I got it all down. The more I saw, the easier it got. One time Montreal tried doing to me what that Montgomery team had done, stack up seven left-handers against me. No problem, I just moved those lefties off the plate, kept them from leaning, then came back outside, and all of a sudden my outside pitch was much more effective, and I was getting myself a whole lot of groundball outs.

Picking up that simple little trick gave me a new dimension as a pitcher. That's the amazing thing about baseball. All those years, and here I was still learning how to pitch.

Part Eight
No Guarantees

A Better Pitcher Than the Year Before

Despite the fine year I'd had in '87, the Mets still weren't ready to guarantee me anything in '88. Here I was, a 34-year-old journeyman pitcher with a doubtful arm and a bargain-basement price tag. Nobody was beating down any doors to pick me up. The Mets had nothing to lose by inviting me back, but I'd have to make the team all over again. Okay, I was used to that kind of treatment. I just rolled up my sleeves and went out and earned myself a spot.

The funny thing is, I thought I was a better pitcher that year than I'd been the year before. My role was back to strictly relief, now. I was kind of disappointed they didn't let me have a single start, after the dozen good ones I'd given them in '87. Maybe they figured I just wasn't strong enough to hold up under the strain of starting on a regular basis. In fact it wasn't even an issue, because that year we had such an awesome starting rotation. Gooden, Darling, Cone, Ojeda, Fernandez — those five guys stayed healthy all year and won 77 games for us. We ended up winning 100 and running off with the East like it was our private property.

I got into 52 games and went 7-2 with a 2.52 e.r.a. My innings-pitched dropped off from 131 to 92, but that was because I was coming out of the bullpen. I sure was busy — Davey had me working my tail off all year. Roger McDowell and I handled the mid-to-later parts of the game, setting up for Randy Myers. A couple of times when Randy was unavailable I went out at the end of games and held the fort, picked up three saves that way. I had a little bit of a rough spot the first month, which I smoothed out after getting a tip from Mel Stottlemyre. Mel noticed I wasn't driving off my right leg and dragging my right knee on the ground the way I have to do to make my submarine pitches effective. From then on I was lights out. All around, that was about as solid a season of pitching as I'd had in the National League.

We went on into the league championship against the Dodgers. Going into that series everybody had us figured as the superior team. During the regular season we'd beaten them ten times in eleven tries. But you can never tell which way those baseball gods are going to be leaning. The Dodgers were in the middle of one of those streaks where you get so hot you get lucky. They were like a fluke team that could do no wrong.

We started out our playoff series against them in decent fashion. Doc held them down pretty well in the first game out in L. A., kept us close until we finally broke through in the ninth and won it. That was how this was supposed to go. But the Dodgers jumped all over David Cone in the second game. We were down five runs before we knew it. I came in and held them scoreless through the sixth and seventh. That's the kind of thing I'd been doing all year, and a lot of times we'd come back to win those games. But in this one we never came back.

We flew home and they beat us two out of three at Shea. The one that really took it out of us was game four. Doc started it for us but went out in the ninth inning. Kirk Gibson won it with a dinger off McDowell in the twelfth. Now the series was locked up at two games apiece. Davey threw Sid Fernandez out there to pitch game five. We pretty much had to have that game. They lit up Sid for three runs in the fifth. I was warming up in the sixth, but before the call came Sid had given up a three-run dinger to Gibson. At that point we were down 6-0. Davey hustled me in there to lock the barn door, but the horse was already out.

We flew out to California again. Now it was do or die. David Cone threw a beauty in game six to keep us alive. It all came down to one game. I was still hungry for my first ring, I'd have been happy to take the ball for them. Instead Davey went to Ron Darling. I had no problem with that. Ronnie was a hard-working pitcher, I figured he'd give them a battle. Ronnie didn't get out of the second inning. At that point we were in trouble, somebody had to ride to the rescue. Now that was a spot I'd excelled in — picking up for a starter who goes out early.

But Davey brought in Doc Gooden. Even today, I still don't understand that. Doc was working on only two days' rest. We had a real strong relief squad that had carried the burden all season. You had Roger McDowell out there, and me.... Well, instead they went to Doc, who hadn't ever pitched in relief. Not a single inning in his entire big league career. Now, it's not that easy to get ready, if you're a starting pitcher. Normally Doc took close to fifteen minutes to warm up; he was a starting pitcher and he was used to doing it that way, but here he didn't have that kind of time. It would have taken McDowell or me about two minutes. We could have gone right in there and cut off that little problem, the way we'd been doing all year. As it was, by the time Doc got loose the Dodgers had five runs across in that second inning, and now our problem was a large one.

I did end up coming into that game, once again too late. I picked up Doc, pitched a scoreless fifth and sixth, but we lost 6-0. My National League championship series stats, all compiled that year, don't look too bad: five innings, zero runs. Still, getting passed over in the second inning of that seventh game did smart a little. I wanted a chance to go out there and get after that ring.

No Guarantees

After going 18-3 over the previous two seasons, I finally got myself a guaranteed contract in 1989. Only one I ever had, in my whole career. I was pretty happy, I didn't have to worry for one year. That's what I thought.

At that point I was banking on being a mainstay in New York for a number of years to come. After all, I'd done everything they'd ever asked me. I'd certainly never given them any trouble. I'd pitched consistently well. When they'd said start, I'd started. If they needed relief, I relieved. I didn't complain, I wasn't highly paid, I accepted that middle-relief role and kept my mouth shut. Remember, this is New York we're talking about. How many guys like me do you find playing on teams from New York? A guy who does well, who doesn't get himself into trouble, doesn't pop off to the newspapers — I had to figure that would be exactly what they would want.

Well, in '89 they started trading away the whole 1986 World Series team, basically. Aguilera got traded, Mookie Wilson, Lenny Dykstra.... But before any of those guys went, I did. I was the guy who'd always stayed in line, picked them up, bailed them out — now here when they were breaking the team up, I was the first guy to go. Nobody should mix up gratitude and the business end of baseball, ever. Even once you've got yourself a guaranteed contract the next thing you have to learn is how much is never going to be guaranteed.

They Don't Appreciate You Till You're Gone

They didn't appreciate me in New York till I was gone. While I was there, they never did seem to pay much attention to me. Almost like they didn't care. I guess it's like they say, the old squeaky wheel gets the oil. Maybe if I'd have been a troublemaker, I'd have got myself noticed. It's like Wally Backman used to say, "Leach is our Rodney Dangerfield." Sometimes it did feel like that — I mean, *I get no respect!*

What's funny is that I think they *did* miss me once I was gone, around the clubhouse at least. I later played in Minnesota with Kevin Tapani, who'd come up to the Mets after I left. Kevin told me there had been a small clubhouse debate in New York over whether or not he should get to have my old number, number 26. Evidently there were some people who wanted to hold that number out, in my honor. And then I also got told a little story about Jeff Innis, another pitcher who'd gone up to the Mets a little after I left. He was a sidearmer, too. He started pitching for them, coming sidearm, and all of a sudden the guys would be all over him, telling him how Leachie used to do things just a little bit differently. It was Leachie this, Leachie that. Leachie's way was the right way. Things haven't been the same since Leachie left. "It was amazing," Jeff said. "*Every* day your name came up in that Mets clubhouse somewhere. Finally I said to them, 'Well, *why* did you get rid of Leach anyway? Why don't you just get him back if you can't get along without him?'"

Addition by Subtraction

You never know what's in people's minds — or anyway in general managers'. Frank Cashen, the man responsible for shipping me out of New York, got asked one time later on why he'd traded me away. "Sometimes you do addition by subtraction," was Frank's reply. What did he mean by that? Hell if I know. He never said that to me. Do you add to your team by subtracting a guy who did whatever you needed? That's funny arithmetic, to me.

How much was I worth to the Mets? For unloading their "insurance policy" all they got was one of those proverbial players to be named later — a minor league pitcher who they picked up at the end of the season and dumped again a year later.

I was surprised all right, when the deal came down. We were on a trip out to Pittsburgh. We'd just landed. It was lunchtime when Davey told me the news. I think he felt kind of strange about it. He'd have had good reason to.

Savannah had been born one month prematurely on May 24 of that year. It wasn't an easy delivery, Chris had to have a C-section. I'd been unable to be there because we were playing in California. I was all night on a flight from the West Coast, trying to get home in time. Chris and Savannah had to stay in intensive care for a while. The team gave me maybe a day to stay with them, then I had to get back out to California to play in a game. I took off for the ballpark, then came back home for three days. We got Savannah out of intensive care the last day of that homestand, a Sunday morning. We brought the baby home from the hospital, and then I had to turn around and take off again that afternoon. We flew out and played a three-game series somewhere, then we went into Pittsburgh. It was the ninth of June.

We'd checked into our hotel and I was out eating lunch with some of the other players. Davey hunted around a little till he found me. It wasn't too hard, in that town there'd only be two or three different places where we'd be. Davey came up to me and said there was something he needed to tell me face-to-face. My stomach got weak when he said that. I said to myself, "Oh Lord, I'm released again."

Instead he told me I was traded. Man, it was a relief. I was going over to the American League, to Kansas City, he told me. So my second thought, after getting over the shock, was, Man, an old guy like me, at my age I'm getting sent off to play in a league that I don't know anything about!

Life in The American League

Before taking off for Kansas City I talked a little bit with Rusty Staub about what it was like over there in the American League. I was a little concerned about all the things I was unfamiliar with. Now Rusty had had eighteen years in the National League, five years in the American League — I figured he ought to know *something*. Rusty said it was all just baseball, you know, just keep playing. So I took that advice. I went on over there and tried to keep an open mind and hoped it was going to be good for me.

Well, it turned out I didn't have too much to be worried about. I ended up staying in the American League longer than I had in the National League. In fact probably my most effective single season of pitching came over there, with the White Sox in 1992. I think I adjusted to the different ways they did things without a whole lot of trouble.

I hate to say this, but I even got to where I *liked* the designated hitter rule. Of course, that was for purely selfish reasons. Now I still believe having pitchers hit is the way the game should be played. That's the proper way, kids should be taught that way. But it sure is easier on a pitcher who's along a bit in his career, when all of a sudden he discovers he doesn't have to run the bases.

You know, over in the National League I'd be hitting and every now and then I'd get myself that fluke double. Once in a while I couldn't help myself, I'd just drop one in. I'd have to bust it around first, dive into second, land on my belly, knock all the breath out of my lungs, choke on dust and get my uniform filthy. The next guy would make a quick out and I'd be standing there on second, still not able to breathe. I'd be totally worn out, but I'd have to go right back and start pitching again.

Now over here in the American League, I found out that a veteran pitcher like Mr. Thirty-five-year-old Terry Leach got treated like a king. You run out, you pitch, you run back in, you sit down. I did have to admit there was something to be said for it.

Two Saves in One Night

My first year in the American League, 1989, was not my best. The new situations and surroundings did take some getting used to. When you're traded and you've got a family, there's plenty of stuff to think about. We had the new baby, I had to move everybody out to Kansas City. Then when we got out there I'd be tired at home, from being up during the middle of the night as a new father. And then at the same time I was meeting my new teammates and trying to fit in. I got caught up in trying to hang out with the guys too much. I had a fun time, I enjoyed those guys, they were super people. But then I'd be tired at home, tired at the ballpark. I just wasn't taking proper care of myself, wasn't getting my rest, and I wasn't as strong as I should have been.

The Royals had a pretty good team. We kept chasing Oakland all summer. Made one pretty good run at the A's toward the end there, but then fell back and came up second, seven games behind them. They went on to be world champs, so we didn't have to feel too bad. We had George Brett still playing, Bo Jackson having a tremendous year. And some outstanding pitching — Saberhagen was just awesome. They had me working mostly long relief, setting up Steve Farr, but I was also used everywhere from late innings to spot starting. They threw me out there to start three times, first taste I'd had of that since '87. I did an okay job of starting — a win, a loss, a no-decision.

I pitched in 30 games after getting there in June, finished up 5-6 with a 4.15 e.r.a. If you look at the numbers, that would be an average year for most guys, but for me it was a little below what I knew I could do. The one occasion that year when I really stepped up and did something out of the ordinary, I guess, was the time I had two saves in one night.

That was one rainy Missouri night out at the ballpark. We got out in front and then there was a long rain delay. When the game got started up again they needed a fresh pitcher to come in and take over. I came in and held the fort the rest of the way. After the game, here came those heavy rains again. I was living over on the Kansas side, in Overland Park, so I had to be driving home on the interstate. Now it's after midnight and pouring down rain. All of a sudden here comes a car down the other side of the highway, out of control, skidding right off the road into the median. That didn't look good. I turned around and came back to see if I could help. The people in that car were in some trouble. A guy with his pregnant wife — she was stuck inside, he and I were trying to get her out. There was nobody else around to help. Right about now, here came another car skidding into the median toward us. And then another one! There was a gentle little curve in the road right at that point, and every car that came around it was hydroplaning and going off the road. One car actually skidded all the way across the median and ended up on the other side of the interstate. It was pretty crazy.

With a lot of pushing and shoving around in the mud we finally managed to get the girl out of that first car. I had slipped and fallen down in that slop at one point, and now I noticed my Triple-A World Series ring, which I was used to wearing all the time, was no longer on my hand. It was pitch dark, everything was sopping wet. I went down on my hands and knees, fishing around in mud and water till I found that ring. Only ring I'd so far got, I wasn't letting go of it that easy. Finally help came. I took the driver of that original car on back to get a tow truck to come and pull his car out. We got to talking a little, and he told me they'd just moved to that area from somewhere out in the country where he hadn't been able to make a living. And now this happens — he was just having all sorts of troubles that night. Well, I was glad to be able to help him out. That's what I mean by getting two saves in one night.

April Fool

In 1990 there was a lockout, so spring training was shortened to three weeks. Right down near the close of camp, Kansas City released me. In case I was tempted to feel too comfortable, here was my reality check — I was thirty-six years old now and getting more vulnerable to the whims of the baseball gods every day.

The Royals cut me on April Fool's Day. Well, things happen for a reason. We were still down in Florida at the time. I had an agent now, so right away he got ahold of a couple of teams. Minnesota showed some interest. Four or five days after Kansas City let me go I went over to the Twins' camp for a tryout. Tom Kelly, the Minnesota manager, took me down to the bullpen. When we got down there Tom acted like a batter and had me pitch to him. He made his judgment about me on the basis of that.

I guess Tom Kelly liked what he saw. I had the ball moving well that day, nice control, everything looking strong. The next day the Twins called me and said, how about coming up to Minnesota? So I flew on up there. When I checked into the hotel, there was a message to call Bobby Valentine down in Texas. Bobby was managing the Rangers at the time. I called him, and he said he was very interested in signing me. Texas was actually offering me a little more money than Minnesota was.

I thought it through pretty carefully. My main objective was to start out the season as well as I could — a good start, and you're probably going to stay. The Rangers were going to be starting the season out on the East Coast playing some teams I had not had much success against. The Twins were starting out on the West Coast, where I'd had pretty good success. That one little thing helped me make my decision.

So I took a little less money and signed with the Twins, and things went just about how I planned. I did really well out West at the beginning of that year. I won a couple of games, didn't give up an earned run in my first thirteen innings. Rick Aguilera was the closer over there now, and they started depending on me as his setup man. I'd secured myself a job. And then as time went by I was even more sure I'd made the right choice between the two deals I'd been offered, because a lot of good things happened to me while I was up there in Minnesota. That first year I was there we came in dead last, but things turned around the next year and I got to go to my first World Series.

I Expand My Repertoire

I got into fifty-five games for Minnesota my first year, 1990 — worked 81 innings and finished up with a 3.20 e.r.a., second best on the Twins' staff after Rick Aguilera. Got into fifty more games in '91, once again pitching exclusively in that middle-relief role that was now getting to be my regular niche.

In those years I learned quite a bit about pitching, mainly out of necessity. Having to adapt to the different strike zone in the American League forced me to experiment around and come up with a couple of new pitches. It was really the first time I'd had to expand my basic repertoire since adopting my submarine delivery down at Savannah ten years before.

Getting used to the strike zone was my biggest adjustment as a pitcher in the new league. I'd heard the umpires did not call balls and strikes the same way over here, and now I was getting to see it. Coming from the National League I was accustomed to a wide and low strike zone. Over here it was narrow and high. In the American League, you did not get those strikes on the outside corner down around the knees. Over here, you had to be in closer, and up a little bit higher, it seemed. Where I was used to working down and away, now they were moving me up and in. Right there, they were forcing me up into a serious hitting zone.

That skinny little American League strike zone used to be a laughing matter between Rick Aguilera and me. "Do you think they could possibly make the thing any narrower?" Rick used to say. "They just squeeze you to death over here." Over in the National League, where we'd both broken in and spent the greater part of our careers, all you had to do was just brush that outside corner and the umps would give it to you. If you were consistent at hitting it, they knew that was your zone, and they would call that strike. That's what we'd been used to. In the American League, there was no way you could get that. I guess maybe after you'd been in their league a while, they'd spread it out for you a bit — but in the beginning over there, all I got was that stingy little welcome wagon squeeze.

To deal with that I felt like I had to come up with a couple of new tricks. For all these years I'd been getting by with the same basic two-pitch repertoire. I had my two-seam sinking fastball, which I threw down and in to right-handers to get groundballs, and then mostly out and away to left-handers. And then I had my slider, which I threw to right-handers whenever I caught them starting to try to turn on the inside fastball, and to left-handers when I wanted to jam them inside on their fists.

Just by experimenting, playing around, I found myself a couple of new pitches. I developed my special slider — a slider that would break *up* at a left-handed hitter. That pitch would come in at their hands and go up right across the inside corner towards their face. Let me tell you, that pitch would light up a few eyes, because a lot of those American League hitters had never seen anything like that before. I'd first stumbled on it by pure accident over in the National League, just fooling around with my regular slider, cutting one or two that went up — and Al Jackson, my Mets pitching coach, said, "Why don't you keep working on that, it's pretty good." Well, over here in the American League I worked on that special slider quite a bit, and eventually it turned into something *nasty*. I'd cut up under that slider and let it ride up in there on those left-handers to move them back off the plate. That allowed me a little room to work with on the outside part of the plate — it had the effect of giving me my outside corner back again.

And then up in Minnesota I also started playing around a little bit with a change-up, which I'd never really tried to throw seriously. That was another idea for dealing with some of those overeager American League hitters who were sitting on their high fastballs. Give them a little air to mash at. Going into '91, I talked the Twins into letting me put a change-up into my mix a little bit in spring training. I think that season I threw about a half dozen change-ups in game situations. I still wasn't really confident about it yet. The next spring, when I was over in spring training with Montreal, Joe Kerrigan, the pitching coach of the Expos, helped me work out a better grip on it, and that improved it a lot. When I went to the White Sox in '92, that change-up was a very effective pitch for me. If I'd kept on working at it and not blown out my elbow again, it might have added a couple more years to my career.

Great Team, No Credit

From last-place losers to world champs in a year is some jump. Did the Twins camp in the spring of '91 show signs of good things to come? I do believe it did. First of all, we all got down there to a brand new spring complex at Fort Myers where everything was bright, shiny and clean. Just the look and feel of that place was enough to give everybody a great fresh attitude right off the bat, and the team seemed to keep that good attitude going all through the spring. We played every game in spring training not just to be getting it over with but to *win* it. You could see something special going on, right at that point there. Just working out and getting themselves into shape wasn't going to be good enough for that team, they weren't going to settle for anything but winning. And the makings of a winner certainly was there. A bunch of really great *team* players — Chili Davis, Kent Hrbek, Brian Harper, Dan Gladden, Al Newman, and probably the best all-round player I ever had the pleasure to play with, Kirby Puckett. We won about twenty-five out of thirty games down there in Florida, so that showed us what we could do. Winning in the spring kind of set a precedent. From then on we felt we had the stuff to go all the way.

When we started out the season, there was a little bit of a hitch. We lost seven out of our first nine and all of a sudden some people were looking kind of down. Steve Bedrosian, a guy I'd played with at Savannah back when we were both in the Braves' system, was one of the veterans with the Twins that year, and he called a team meeting at the hotel bar in Seattle. Bedrock said a couple of things and then we had a small party. All got together and laughed and cut up, got a little rowdy. That kind of loosened up the whole group a little bit. Right after that we started winning again.

This time we never stopped. It was just a great year. We hogged first place the whole way, stayed ahead of everybody. Nobody took us seriously. We'd go around beating everybody, but somehow we couldn't get any respect. The conventional wisdom was that we were just holding first place until somebody else who was more deserving of it came up and overtook us. We didn't care what got said, we just kept on winning. At one point we ran off a fifteen-game winning streak. The sixteenth game, we were ahead in the ninth, but Aguilera let it get away — one of the very few times he did that all year. Some people thought we might crack, then. We came back and won the next two games after that. That was our trademark, we didn't let anything get us down.

We *knew* we had a great team, even though nobody would give us credit. It wasn't too hard to understand why not. We were coming off a last-place season, we were playing in a small town, we got no publicity, nobody wrote about us. The attention was always going elsewhere. All you ever heard about was Oakland. Oakland was going to catch us, Oakland was going to beat us. Well, after a while we were a little tired of hearing about that. *Nobody* could catch us that season. Oakland finished in fourth place, buried eleven games deep in our dust as we won going away.

The Five Percent Solution

We clinched the pennant about the third week of September. By that time, the roster limits had been expanded, and we were carrying a couple of extra players. Now it came down to who would make the post-season roster. Of course, some guys didn't have to worry about that: they weren't about to cut Kirby Puckett. Me, I was a veteran of the numbers game, and couldn't afford to take anything for granted.

When I got out to the ballpark one night I was told the G. M., Mr. MacPhail, wanted to see me up in his office. My first thought was, Oh no, they're not releasing me? Then I thought a little bit more, and it got a little bit better — maybe he wanted to extend my contract. Well, I went on up. Mr. MacPhail told me where things stood. He explained that Allan Anderson, who'd been having an off-year and gone down to Triple-A and now had come back up, was very likely going to be put on the post-season roster in my place. There was a ninety-five percent probability they were leaving me off. That left me a five percent chance.

I was real bummed out, I can tell you. Here we were going to the playoffs. I'd thought maybe I was finally going to be getting my shot at earning myself a ring. That night, I was sitting down in the bullpen mulling all this over, when our starter got himself into some trouble in the middle innings and somebody had to get ready. That would normally have been my spot to warm up, but they got Allan up instead. And then the call came, and in he went. I guess they were giving him his dress rehearsal for the playoffs right there. Well, Allan had a tough time of it that night. He was a starting pitcher, he wasn't used to that kind of hurry-up-and-get-ready role, and he got knocked around.

I think that got Tom Kelly to thinking. Allan was a starter, not a reliever. In the post-season you've got all those days off, you don't need that extra starter as much as you need a reliever. I'd been *trained* as a reliever. The next day, I walked into the clubhouse, there's T. K. standing in the middle of the room, holding this riding-crop. He saw me and pointed me into his office with it. I said, "Oh Jeez. I'd just as soon they'd horsewhip me as drop me off the roster."

Got into the office, Tom closed the door. Mr. MacPhail was in there. He says, "Well, Tom's been using that riding-crop on me. You remember that five percent chance? It looks like the longshot came in."

Did that perk up my spirits a little? I could hardly contain myself, I was so happy. Just so fired up, I could have gone out and run a hundred miles. As it was, I told Tom Kelly I was very grateful to him. I knew it was Tom I had to thank for my five percent solution.

We went on to the playoffs against Toronto. Split two games at home, then went on up to Canada to play them three games up there. That was the one place we'd played poorly all year, Toronto. People said we'd be doing well just to win one game and survive up there. We beat them all three games. Our starting pitchers were so good, I wasn't even needed. The final game, the one time our starter struggled, David West went in early and just blew people away through the middle innings, then Carl Willis came on and set up Aguilera. Boom, it was all over and I hadn't even got a chance to play.

There was plenty of celebrating after we'd won that game and the league championship, but personally I still wasn't satisfied. I told Carl Willis, "If T. K. doesn't find some way to get me into that World Series, I'm going to pin him up against the wall and make him!" I hadn't come this far just to be sitting down in the bullpen.

The Tunnel (World Series, 1991)

We went into the World Series up against the Braves. Our starters and Aguilera stayed hot and we won the first two games at home. Still no work for me. The third game in Atlanta, Tom Kelly finally did put me in, though not quite under the circumstances I was hoping for. Pitching in that kind of pressure is like stepping up to a different level of baseball. My idea was, bring me in to start an inning, when it's nice and calm, so I can just kind of work my way into things and get myself settled down. Instead here it's bases loaded, two outs, bottom of the fifth, Atlanta up 4-1 and the whole house rocking with the Tomahawk Chop.

When I joined Tom Kelly out at the mound I looked up and gave my first thought to who I was going to be facing. The hitter was Mark Lemke, a left-hander. Lemke hit .417 in that Series, he was hitting just out of his mind. Normally I am about the *last* pitcher you would bring in with the bases loaded against a left-handed hitter who is really raking the ball. Standing out there on the mound with the whole of Atlanta Stadium going nuts doing all that chanting and chopping, I was tempted to ask T. K., "Do you know what you're *doing* here, Tom? You're bringing a sidearmer in against a left-hander. You *never* do that. I mean, what are you *thinking* about here?" But I didn't say a word. With all that noise, Tom never would have heard me.

I had about thirteen friends up in the stands that night, people who had come over from Selma. I'd managed to get tickets for them all. Afterwards they were asking, "Man, weren't you nervous out there, weren't you scared? Because that was the loudest at-bat of the whole game. Those people were rocking so loud we thought they were going to bring down the grandstand."

Well, to be honest with you, I don't remember hearing any noise at all at that moment. I was kind of floating, hyperventilating a little bit I guess. All I remember is T. K. talking to me, mouthing his usual gruff "Go get 'em, do the best you can" — which I couldn't so much *hear* as *see* him saying — and then patting me on the back and walking off. And then the next thing I recall is seeing Brian Harper, my catcher, standing there at home plate. Brian, a left-handed hitter, the umpire and me — there was a tunnel right there, absolutely quiet, and all of us were in it.

I pretty much threw finesse out the window and just reared back and let that first pitch go, hoping somehow it would turn out to be a strike. It was. That gave me something to build on. I threw all fastballs. If I mixed one slider in there, I don't remember it now. My four pitches to Mark Lemke with the bases loaded were all strikes. Strike one, strike two, then one he fouled off, then one he swung at and missed for strike three. I was just real happy to get on and off the field — I'd done what I'd been sent out there to do, and I just wanted to go sit down.

We lost that one and eventually got swept down there in Atlanta. In game five I got to pitch two more innings. That time I did give up a run. Took a bolt off my leg, ow! It hurt plenty later, but at the time it barely stung me. A run came in, but no big deal. My second inning of work I was just right. Back in my groove, a three-up, three-down inning. I'd just had to calm down. Now I was into it. My heart was going about a hundred miles an hour. I was ready to pitch for four or five more innings, if they'd asked me. Hell, I could have pitched all night. But I left for a pinch hitter, and Bedrosian and Willis came in and got punished. They blew us out, 14-5.

All we wanted to do after that game was get out of Atlanta and out of sight and earshot of that crazy chopping and chanting. Three nights of that would drive anybody half nuts. That stuff bothered us a lot more than losing the ballgames. There was even a bunch of maniacs lined up outside our bus as we came out of the stadium, they had a tomahawk chop going and were screaming their fool heads off. This was really getting old!

Atlanta still had one last shot saved up for us. We rode that bus out to the airport, hauled ourselves up on board this big old Delta jet. We were taxiing down the runway, picking up speed to take off. I had a window seat, and I noticed something off to my left. A little Delta Airlines truck was barreling down the margin of the runway alongside us — just *flying* along next to us, trying to keep up. And dang if there weren't two idiots on that truck doing a tomahawk chop for our benefit. I said, "Let us get *out* of here!"

Even though we'd lost those three games in Atlanta, once that plane got off the ground our spirits lifted right back up. We weren't even worried. It was like we had no doubt what we were going to accomplish when we got back home. Everybody seemed very confident — Kirby Puckett, Kent Hrbek, none of our main guys was looking the least bit down. Getting blown out in that last game had almost made it easier on us, in a funny way. We weren't going to chew over that, we weren't even going to remember it.

Back in Minnesota we got two great-pitched games from Scott Erickson and Jack Morris. Puck won the sixth game with an eleventh inning home run, Morris pitched a ten-inning shutout to win game seven. Then we could party for real.

How much fun was all that? Don't even ask me. I was so happy. To be with a bunch of guys who've worked hard all year together and then to win the World Series — well, in my fifteen years in the game I had a lot of good moments, but that was definitely the best.

It was doubly great to be sharing it with my wife Chris, because I definitely think she had something to do with it. All that season, every night she'd prayed that I'd be able to get to go to the World Series — not because the World Series meant that much to her, but because she always wanted me to have what I wanted to have, and she knew that was something I'd wanted my whole life.

After the Series, we all got to the White House. Made sure I got on TV. Oh, I was riding high! It probably wasn't until I went back to Selma that fall that the whole thing really started to sink in. They had a ceremony for me back there, the mayor of Selma gave a little speech and the town changed the name of our old baseball stadium, where I'd pitched in high school, to Terry Leach Field. I was very taken by that, couldn't hold back a tear or two as a matter of fact. My folks were there, all the people who'd known and supported me over the years. What a homecoming that was.

A New Home

So now in the spring of '92 I could start my big league World Series jewelry collection going for real, with the ring I was getting from the Twins. (The ring that was still due to me from the '86 Mets I wasn't actually able to pick up till three years after this, as I've explained.) What I didn't have that spring, however, was a job. After the '91 Series the Twins showed their appreciation for the good job I'd done, in typical baseball-business fashion. They didn't sign me back. I was out of work again, a situation which by then I was a lot more familiar with than I'd have liked to be.

That was the spring Eddie Haas hooked me up with Montreal. The Expos signed me and I went to spring training with them. The idea was, they wanted to see if my arm was still strong enough to go out and pitch every other day or so, the way you have to do over in the National League — where because they don't have the DH rule they're going to need more relief innings. Well, I pitched in at least fifteen games for them that spring, and I thought I was really showing them something. I'll bet you I wasn't averaging more than eight or nine pitches an inning, that's how easily I was breezing along. I mean I was really on. I was feeling great. Everything looked just fine.

I didn't know the Expos were still out shopping. First they made a trade with the Mets to pick up a left-hander, then they signed up a closer who'd been released by Pittsburgh. Come to find out the first guy didn't pitch for them much that year. The closer was making $1.8 million and got hurt, so they didn't keep him around very long. But once they'd made those two deals, there was suddenly a surplus of arms. If you've been paying attention so far, you can probably guess which 38-year-old gray-haired relief pitcher had to go, when the roster limit came down. It was too bad. Montreal had a pretty good team that year, they were trying to put something together. They came in second, as it turned out. Who knows how much further a little extra pitching might have taken them? Instead they got rid of a guy who wasn't costing them much and who could have helped them. Where's the sense in that? You tell me.

Here I was, a free agent again. The week the season started, the White Sox gave me a call. I went over to Chicago and proved to people that my great spring with the Expos had not been just a mirage.

When I first got over there, it seemed like the people in Chicago really didn't know much about me. Gene Lamont, the manager — a very nice man, by the way — sat me down and talked to me about what my role would be. The main middle-relief spot down there was already taken by Donn Pall, who'd done a pretty good job for them the year before. I was going to be mop-up guy. If the game was tied or close or we were ahead in the middle innings when a starter came out, Donn Pall would get the nod. If we were behind, it would be me.

Well, I hated that, but what was I going to do? I went out and pitched in a whole lot of games when we were behind. Did okay at that, but then it got to where I developed a little phobia. The problem didn't appear until I'd worked my way up the ladder and they were putting me into games when we were ahead. I've always liked to pitch with a lead, but now all of a sudden pitching with a lead was difficult for me, because I would try to be too fine. I didn't want to get dropped back into the mop-up role. That little worry would be in the back of my mind. Trying too hard would mess me up, I'd lose concentration and give up a base hit or walk somebody.

A little more work, and I just relaxed and got over it. Once I stopped worrying and just approached things my normal way, instead of trying to do too much, everything went okay again.

By the end of the year the White Sox were using me in tight situations, tie games, extra-inning games on the road where there was no margin of error at all — situations where you knew if you didn't cut it you probably wouldn't get a second chance. I loved it. I did a whole lot of pitching for them, finally. We were trying to hang in there in a little race with Oakland and Minnesota, and by the end of the '92 season it was getting to where I was being leaned on to do more and more, and I was solid as a rock. We ended up in third place behind the A's and the Twins, but no one could question my contribution. I got into fifty-one games and ended up with the third-lowest e.r.a. in the league, 1.95 for the season, actually the lowest earned-run average of my big league career.

Toward the end of that year in Chicago some reporter did an interview with our pitching coach, Jackie Brown. The guy asked Jackie who in his eyes was the most valuable pitcher on our staff. Now we had some real star pitchers at the time, Jack McDowell who won twenty games that year, Alex Fernandez, Bobby Thigpen who was the closer. Jackie said, "This may sound stupid, but the MVP of our staff was Terry Leach." When I heard that, I felt like I'd really found a home.

I Tried to Push It and It Snapped

The White Sox won the West in '93, but lost out that year in the playoffs to Toronto. Their bullpen let them down in the last two games of that series. You got the feeling they could have used another arm. Maybe I could have helped them, if I'd been around. As it was, I watched those playoff games from the stands. I had a metal contraption holding my arm together at the time. I'd just been operated on.

I started feeling a little bit of strain in spring training, but I didn't want to let on. I was trying to establish myself as a prominent pitcher with Chicago. Had my eyes on getting myself a little bit of a raise, and a longer contract. My salary was still down near the minimum, at this time. Coming into the '93 season, I asked them for a little more money, based on the real good year I'd just had for them. All I wanted to do was get myself back up closer to the average pay for a guy who'd put in my amount of time. I thought maybe since I'd given them more than they'd expected in '92, they'd be willing to help me out a bit. That didn't work out, so I was thrown back on having to prove myself to them all over again. I figured if I could have another good year in '93 I'd have it made. I was looking ahead, thinking about my future.

In the spring I was throwing very well. Jackie Brown told me I was getting better velocity and movement than I had ever gotten the year before. He said everything looked good — and I was *feeling* great, and pitching really well. But then when the season started, my arm was bothering me a little. I went ahead and tried to pitch through it. Instead of just trying to mellow back and take care of it, I tried to push, get a little more. In my mind I was pitching with my career on the line. I wasn't holding anything back. But then one day in April, I went into a game to Boston and on one pitch I just pushed it a little too hard. Heard that *snap* in my elbow again — knew what it was right away. Seventeen years since I'd heard that sound before, but here, when it happened again, I didn't need but an instant to recognize it. It was like re-living a real old nightmare.

After that it was very hard to come back. I rested and rehabbed my arm for about six weeks, went down to the Triple-A team in Nashville for a while, then came back up to Chicago. Pitched up there with the injury for about a month. The funny thing is I wasn't doing too badly, my numbers were just fine: a 2.81 e.r.a. in fourteen games. You'd think from that stat-line I wasn't having any problems.

In fact when I first got back from rehab I *was* doing really well. If I had just stayed mellow and calm and held back a little, maybe things would have gone okay. But as soon as things were going better again, I started trying to let it out a little harder, a little harder. It snapped again.

Back to the disabled list. It was a *real* tough rehab, that second time around. And I never could get it back that time, it just never worked again. I tried going down and pitching another rehab stint at Nashville. Hurt it again down there. Rested a while, then went up and threw a little batting practice in Chicago. People up there thought I looked great, told me there was nothing wrong with me. I said, "Well, I may look fine right now, but tomorrow I won't be able to throw a baseball." I'd lost all the bounce-back in my arm.

So they sent me on down to Double-A in Birmingham to do another rehab, try to get some strength back. It was September now, they were trying to get me ready so I could help them out down the stretch.

I gave it my best shot in Birmingham, but all my strength was gone. My velocity was down to 74 miles an hour. Still, somehow I was able to get Double-A guys out with a 74-mile-an-hour fastball. The game they clocked me at 74, as a matter of fact, I pitched one inning, threw twelve pitches and struck out all three hitters I faced. On every one of those pitches I had a whole lot of pain in my elbow. There was no point denying it, so I said I was hurting. But here I was getting hitters out. The people in the Chicago organization couldn't understand why I didn't *feel* good. I'd tell them I was getting pain in my arm, and they'd tell me maybe the pain was all in my head. They were practically accusing me of being a head case. I said, "Jeez, I've pitched over a long time, I'm not going to come up a head case here at the end of my career." Okay, I'd been given that little challenge. I went out and tried to turn it up a notch. Threw just one pitch a little harder, and now it snapped again. *Real* bad, this time.

This time the pain was so bad I just had to give up. I told them that was it, I wanted Dr. Andrews to take a look. Dr. Andrews is an orthopedic surgeon down there in Birmingham who probably has as good a knowledge of this kind of injury as any medical man in the world. I went in and had some MRIs and got everything checked out. The tests showed just a small tear in the ligament in my elbow. I was told it could be surgically repaired, but there would be a real long recovery-time. Now there was a big debate. It would be a year and a half for rehab, if I had the surgery. I'd be forty-one years old, trying to make my comeback. I don't believe the White Sox thought too much of my chances. And too, they were looking at what all this was going to cost them. They'd never believed I was really hurting. They weren't in favor of the operation. Well, it was my arm, I knew I was hurt, and I thought if I got things fixed up I could make it back. I wanted to at least give it a shot, I didn't want to just quit. So I went in and had the doctors operate on me.

While the surgery was going on, Dr. Andrews stepped out and talked to my parents. That tear in my elbow was a lot more extensive than anybody had thought, he told them. The ligament was completely severed, there was nothing in there holding it together. And there was a big calcium deposit behind the elbow.

Now none of this damage had showed up on the tests they'd been doing. They'd put me through MRIs, x-rays, bone scans, orthograms, where they inject dyes up there — the whole nine yards. The extent of the problem had just not been showing up.

And here all along I'd had everybody in Chicago, the GM, the management people, asking me over and over, "You sure this is not in your head? You sure you're really hurting?"

I guess the news that turned up during the surgery was both bad and good. My elbow was a mess, but I was vindicated on the charge of making my injury up. During my recuperation I went over and talked to the trainer with the Double-A club. He said, "I've got no idea how you were able to pitch so well with an elbow like that." I said, "All I could tell you is that it *hurt.*"

Looking back at that point, after the surgery, the whole long misery of my '93 season clicked into perspective. There had been a large misunderstanding. The reason nobody had wanted to believe I was really injured was that I'd been able to get batters out. The thing was, I'd done so much work, done so many exercises that I'd developed a certain amount of strength in the support muscles around the injury, and they could function as a kind of backup system, holding the elbow together for a while. But it was like jerry-rigging a dam to hold back a flood. When the arm got tired, those support muscles would start giving out. Then the bone would start just snapping in and out of the socket. It felt like that bone was just clanging around in there, like it was just slipping into the joint and then slamming back out again. So every time I'd try to pitch, it was like going down a step. I'd throw a day or two later, and I'd have a little less strength. Then another day or two and I'd be a little bit lower. Finally I'd hit the bottom step, where there was nothing left. I had no pop. You can't pitch very long without an elbow.

Don't Count Me Out

So that was my '93 season — a major pain. After having the big surgery, I did the big rehab. Came back to Florida and worked very hard with Larry Mayo, who had been the Mets' trainer when I was with them. A very good Christian man, very hard worker. Larry had faith that I could make it. He knew I was a quick healer, because he'd helped me through a rehab with my knee back in '91. He always said the secret of my longevity was being a fast healer. Another one of my secrets was having Larry to work with me.

After that elbow surgery it's normally eighteen months before you can get back on the mound to pitch. I made it in six months. In the spring of '94 I was back throwing again. At that point the Cubs were interested in me, but I had to turn them down. The White Sox had paid for my surgery, so I felt I owed it to them to go back to them. Well, I went back, but it might have been a mistake. I pitched okay for them in spring training. My first time out I had a three-up, three-down inning against Toronto, and I thought I was back. The White Sox gave me seven innings in spring training, then told me they couldn't use me any more. To me, that wasn't right. When a guy has proven his loyalty, he deserves a shot. I felt they should have at least let me go down to Triple-A and get in some work, to see if I couldn't still help them out.

I felt the way Chicago treated me wasn't right, but then again, I had a brand new arm. I had to start to learn pitching all over. That new arm was like a gun. I had to gauge this thing back in, re-calibrate it. I still felt like I could throw. I made a lot of calls, let people know I was on the lookout for work. I kept in shape through a good part of that '94 season, just in case somebody called me back. But nobody did, so finally I went to work with Health South, a rehab hospital firm.

When the spring of '95 rolled around, I was forty-one years old and had been out of the game nearly two years, but my arm felt pretty good and I still thought I could get people out. There was a strike going on that year, in the spring teams were bringing in replacement players. I got four calls about coming back as a replacement player. Well, I told those four teams I couldn't do that, but I *would* be willing to come in to minor league camp and just be a minor league player until the end of the strike. Then I'd be ready and happy to come back up as a major leaguer, once the strike was resolved. The only one of those four teams to take me up on that proposal was Detroit. Detroit sounded interested. I said to myself, "Excellent — Detroit's a good place for me to go, Sparky Anderson's always big into older players." I figured they'd take a look at my past record, see the kind of value I'd given other teams, and know they could expect the same thing out of me now.

I went over to Lakeland and got into a Detroit uniform and had a very good '95 spring training. One of my best springs ever, as it turned out: twenty-four innings, like a one-point-nine e.r.a., walked only three, struck out about fourteen. As strong as I was feeling at that point, I told the Detroit people I thought I could pitch another three or four more years for them at least, maybe five. I actually thought I had a future with them. Well, I never saw Opening Day.

It came down to that same old thing I'd heard all through my career: they were going to go with the younger players. The Detroit people were looking for twenty-three-year-olds, there I was at forty-one. I tried to convince them the record books had it wrong, I was only twenty-nine. Of course that would have had me playing for the Mets when I was fourteen, which would really have been prodigious. No, the pitching end of things was not going to be the problem, it was just my age. My brand new arm was fresh and strong, but the rest of me was gaining fast on Sparky Anderson. Before the end of spring training, Detroit cut me.

Come the next season, 1996, I was still at it. Pitched that year in the thirty-and-over World Series down in Fort Myers, threw a little batting practice to get ready for it, then threw eight innings in the first game I pitched. Two days later I came back and went two innings, two days after that I went three more. I took three days off, then I threw a nine-inning complete game. That's twenty-some innings in just over a week. No pain, my arm never hurt. I mean I wasn't even the least bit sore the day after I'd been throwing. It was almost a miracle, my brand new bionic arm.

The good Lord has his reasons. Did he snap that old elbow for me just so Dr. Andrews could make me a better one? Today, a half dozen years after that surgery, I might just be a better pitcher than I was before. I'm getting the same velocity I had when I was in the big leagues, the same movement, my slider's breaking just as good. Also I'm a lot wiser now, which ought to help any player. In fact there's no reason, other than age prejudice, why I can't be pitching in the big leagues today, in my opinion.

I've settled down with my family in Florida and entered partnership with another ex-player, Tony Ferreira, in a company called Pro-Kids Baseball, Inc. We hold instructional baseball camps for kids. Tony and I got to know each other when we were both with the Mets organization back in '86. He ended up moving down here, and we got a little tradition going where we'd meet up on January 3rd of every year with some other players — Bobby Thigpen, Jesse Orosco, Kip Gross, Ray Searage, sometimes Doc Gooden, Gary Sheffield — and all work out together every day from then on up to spring training, getting ourselves in shape and giving ourselves a bit of a head start. Out of that little seed grew the idea of starting a baseball school together, which Tony and I did back in the spring of '95. We teach kids the fundamentals, how to catch, how to throw. We don't stress winning, but how to play the game. Learn that, and you *will* win. We have two teams, eighteen and under, fifteen and under. We've got both boys and girls — in fact last year the best arm we had out there was on a girl. We try to groom all our kids for moving up to a higher level of baseball, but we recommend very strongly that they get a college education before turning pro. Last year two of our kids got drafted, one of them in the third round, and we were real proud of his achievements, even though he chose not to sign a contract yet and to continue his education at the University of Florida.

I'm forty-five now, but I've kept myself in good shape. I'm on the baseball field with young people every day, all afternoon and on into the night. My arm's feeling fine, and I'm throwing the ball as well as I ever did. In a quiet way I've let it be known lately to a few big league scouts that I'd be willing to try out. So far nobody's taken me up on it. But I'm not giving up yet, so don't you count me out.

Things Happen for a Reason

Regardless of whether I ever get to pitch again in the big leagues, I'm sure now that all my long struggles to make it up there and try to stay were for a reason. There are reasons for everything that's gone on, for why we're here and for what's happening. I think now that the good Lord had his reason way back in 1976 for snapping my elbow in the first place. Being an overhand hard thrower was never going to work for me — if I hadn't been injured in college I'd never have thrown hard enough to get up to the major leagues. He changed me to something that worked, a sidearmer who could give a difficult time to any right-handed hitter who ever walked up to the plate.

Baseball's a frustrating game at times, other times it's exciting, and then again strange, even kind of deep. Spending your life in it, you'll find insecurity, confusion, joy, boredom, friendship, mistrust, surprise, despair, hope and pain. So much happens — you just have to be conscious of the fact that you're not in control of any of it, and from that point on it all does make sense, in a funny kind of way.

Part Nine

Postscript

Reunion Day

To close out this story in a little bit lighter kind of way, let me tell you about one of my nicer baseball experiences of recent years. I hadn't been in any kind of serious ballpark for quite a while before going back to the '96 twenty-year reunion of our Auburn College World Series baseball team. I went on back there and saw a lot of the guys I hadn't seen in twenty years, and we got taken through the new baseball park Auburn had just built. Real nice new park, made me think of Camden Yards in some ways, and also it has a big high green outfield wall like the one at Fenway.

We were going to be having our reunion ceremony and then Auburn was going to be playing a game that day. Before the game us old guys got to take some batting practice. Everybody had a chance to test out their old strokes. To my surprise, quite a few of those guys could still hit a little bit. Got to stand in there against some live pitching myself, and dang if I didn't hit a couple of pretty good shots up on that Green Monster!

We had our little ceremony. They announced the names of players who had made All-Southeastern Conference. Several people had done that, but I was not one of them. You never found me on any All-Star teams anywhere I went, for some reason. But then when the game started, they did surprise me by asking me to throw out the first pitch. I was really happy to do that, and had a great time at it.

I thought I'd do it up right. Went on out and kind of hot-dogged it up a little bit. Acted like I was shaking the catcher off, went into my sidewinder motion, dropped down into a hard sidearm just like I used to do in the major leagues. Man, I could tell most of those people down there hadn't seen much of *that*. I winged a nice little moving, sinking fastball up there, and it popped in the catcher's mitt. That was exactly the pitch I would have thrown that day if you would have asked me to get one man out in a World Series.

I was pretty proud of that reunion day first-ball pitch, I'll have to tell you. Even the TV guys who were announcing the game commented on it, I later heard. They said it looked and sounded like I still had some pretty good velocity. Then when I came down off the mound the coach of the Auburn college team pulled me over. "You happen to have any eligibility left?" Don't look now, but for a second there I was tempted to think he might be serious. "About three innings," I told him. "Okay, be ready, we'll let you know if we need you."

That whole day was just a lot of fun. Got to meet the families of a bunch of my old friends. Once the game was underway we all got to sit in the stands of that nice new stadium and enjoy the view from the closest thing to a big league ballpark that I had been in for quite a while. When we were in college there, the baseball field was nothing but grass, dirt and some rickety bleachers that you sat in up on the side of the hill. Now that day I could just see that old field again in my mind's eye, and then all kinds of other fields and parks I'd been in, too. I remember when I was in the big leagues, sometimes after coming out of a game instead of heading straight for the showers I'd just stay in the dugout and soak it all up, the color of the grass, the stadium, the whole ambience of the game I loved and never wanted to leave. I knew I'd better enjoy it, in the moment, really drink it in, because I might never see it again. So here on reunion day, I got to sit up there in the stands with all of my friends and just talk and laugh and cut up and catch up with them, catch up with all those lost years. Next time, let's all get back together before it's been twenty years again. ∎

Terry Leach • Career Statistics

Yr.	Team	ERA	W	L	SV	IP	G	CG	H	R	ER	BB	SO
73	Auburn	2.14	1	3	0	33.2			33	14	8	24	18
74	Auburn	1.30	9	0		55			26	13	8	29	26
75	Auburn	3.84	5	2		58.2	12	3	51	26	25	27	18
76	Auburn	2.57	8	5		84	15	6	54	34	24	41	71
76	Baton Rouge	6.16	0	1	0	19	5	1	43	21	13	14	15
77	Greenwood	2.55	3	2	3	67	20	0	47	25	19	24	67
78	Savannah	5.04	1	0	0	25	9	0	24	17	14	13	21
78	Kinston	3.27	5	4	8	66	34	0	57	29	24	25	46
79	Savannah	1.96	2	9	2	92	40	0	77	33	20	26	68
79	Richmond	1.93	3	1	1	14	7	1	14	3	3	4	12
80	Savannah	3.66	5	1	1	91	24	2	90	43	37	20	60
80	Jackson	1.50	5	1	0	54	8	3	50	16	9	15	30
81	Jackson	1.71	5	1	0	58	8	2	47	14	11	12	43
81	Tidewater	2.72	5	2	0	76	15	4	63	27	23	19	42
81	Mets	2.57	1	1	0	35	21	0	26	11	10	12	16
82	Tidewater	2.96	4	1	5	49	30	0	48	20	16	19	34
82	Mets	4.17	2	1	3	45.1	21	1	46	22	21	18	30
83	Tidewater	4.46	5	7	6	113	37	2	120	66	56	42	66
84	Richmond	9.20	1	2	1	14.2	12	0	28	16	15	3	6
84	Tidewater	1.90	10	2	0	80.1	31	0	70	26	17	27	53
85	Tidewater	1.59	1	0	4	45.1	24	0	33	12	8	8	25
85	Mets	2.91	3	4	1	55.2	22	1	48	19	18	14	30
86	Tidewater	2.49	4	4	7	79.2	34	1	69	30	22	21	56
86	Mets	2.70	0	0	0	6.2	6	0	6	3	2	3	4
87	Mets	3.22	11	1	0	131.1	44	1	132	54	47	29	61
88	Mets	2.54	7	2	3	92	52	0	95	32	26	24	51
89	Mets	4.22	0	0	0	21.1	10	0	19	11	10	4	2
89	Royals	4.15	5	6	0	73.2	30	0	78	46	34	36	34
90	Twins	3.20	2	5	2	81.2	55	0	84	31	29	21	46
91	Twins	3.61	1	2	0	67.1	50	0	82	28	27	14	32
92	White Sox	1.95	6	5	0	73.2	51	0	57	17	16	20	22
93	White Sox	2.81	0	0	1	16	14	0	15	5	5	2	3
93	Nashville	3.18	0	0	1	5.2	5	0	4	2	2	0	4
93	Birmingham	4.15	0	0	1	4.1	4	0	4	2	2	2	5

Major League Totals	ERA	W	L	SV	IP	G			R	ER	BB	SO
	3.15	38	27	10	699.2	376			279	245	197	331

Chris, Savannah, and Terry Leach.

Tom Clark's writings on baseball have won him cult-classic status as a "Major League Author," to take a phrase from a trading card series in which he is featured. With 1970s pitching star and folk hero Mark "The Bird" Fidrych he co-authored the memoir *No Big Deal,* hailed by Jonathan Yardley in *Sports Illustrated* as "the funniest sports book of the year" in 1976. His 1978 *One Last Round for the Shuffler* won belated tribute for unearthing from research in Southern local history the true story of a blacklisted major-league pitcher of the 1920s, Shufflin' Phil Douglas. Baseball writer/poet Donald Hall has called Clark's 1975 account of the rise and fall of Charles Finley's Oakland A's *(Champagne and Baloney)* "the great neglected sports book of our time." Clark's baseball poetry (including *Fan Poems,* North Atlantic Books, 1976) and his baseball paintings of the same period are now legendary.

Clark is also recognized as a poet, novelist, literary critic, and biographer. He has written acclaimed "lives" of the American writers Damon Runyon, Jack Kerouac, and Charles Olson, and is currently at work on *Edward Dorn: The Last Range.*